RELATIONSHIP WORKBOOK FOR COUPLES

Would you like to meet your soul mate? In these pages, you will discover the deepest reasons that can hinder the realization of your dream.

Julia & Julio

TABLE OF CONTENTS

Introduction

Congratulations on downloading **Relationship workbook for couples** and thank you for doing so. If this text, as we hope, will be to your liking, we would like a comment containing your thought…

The following chapters will discuss; Who is a Soul mate, Decisions that influence the choice of a soul mate, Boundaries before choosing a soul mate, what complicates a relationship before it becomes official, Communication in a relationship, and Finding your soul mate.

You may have heard about meeting a soul mate and giggled, because you thought it's an illusion. The book starts by explaining who a soul mate is. It further tells you the qualities of a soul mate because, you can meet your soul mate and they are out there waiting for you. You will also learn on how you can identify a soul mate.

There are boundaries that you should adhere to before choosing a soul mate. You will learn more on what to do before you meet them, and unconscious decisions could kill your dream to meeting a soul mate. The book will also teach you some of the decisions that influence your choice of a partner. Did you know some decisions you make kill the relationship before you make it official? Well, read through to find out.

Every healthy relationship needs good communication. It's crucial in building a successful partnership. Poor communication is one of the relationship killers. The book will tell you more on the dos and don'ts relating to communication.

Finally, you can meet your soul mate but at the wrong time. The book tells you more about the wrong timing. Further, you will get insight on what to do when you find them.

There are plenty of books on this subject on the market, thanks again for choosing this one! Every effort was made to ensure it is full of as much useful information as possible, please enjoy!

Chapter One

INTRODUCTION TO A SOUL MATE

Who is a soulmate?

A soulmate is a person who is aligned with your soul. There is a feeling of deep natural affinity. A soul mate could be termed as an ideal partner. That whose connection flows with yours and gets you. Maybe the next thing you may ask yourself is how do you find your soul mate? You may have heard a lot about people saying they are waiting for their soul mate. This may have you wondering if it happens or it's just an illusion. Well, soul mates do exist. Soulmates are connected naturally. Your soulmate is easy to talk to. It's more than love at first sight.

Identifying your soulmate

You may want to start exploring and keen to identify your soulmate. It is important to note that a soulmate is not a one-sided relationship. It is a heart to heart connection. You can tell that you have met your soulmate if you note the following;

You have deep mindset chemistry: Soulmates read the mind of each other and you may even complete each other's sentences. You may have incidences where you say the same things at the same time. Soulmates communicate without speaking. A soulmate knows how to act in response to your emotional signals. They stay close when you open your heart to them, give you their undivided attention and comfort you when in need. Basically, a soulmate knows how to answer to your needs.

You are connected spiritually: Everything flows smoothly without forcing it. It feels like a person you have known all your life. You allow yourself to be vulnerable around them. You are free to take the risk and share your emotions comfortably.

You have a deep desire to forever stay with this person: You never get bored while around them. There is a gut feeling that confirms to you that you have found the one!

You both have a naturally deep respect for each other: Despite the challenges that you encounter, there is still the strong bond. Finding a soulmate is not a guarantee that there are no challenges, but rather the challenges strengthen the relationship.

You are at peace with them: They calm your spirit. Peace comes with a feeling that you got each other for the long term. Most of the time, while in a wrong relationship, there is a sense of insecurity. However, with a soulmate, you feel inner assurance that the relationship is right and healthy.

The person inspires and encourages you to improve yourself: Soulmates help you grow as an individual. This is someone who sees the potential in you and encourages you to be better every day. They don't judge you or limit your possibilities.

You feel that they came just at the right time: You may have known each other before, but you are ready for the next level just at the same time. Your soul mates maybe your former school mate and after a long period, you meet and feel like you are meant for each other. You need to be open to meeting your soulmate.

Qualities of a soulmate

We all hold different ideas and dreams of love. You may want your ideal partner maybe good looking, while I want the one who doesn't lie. You have the deal breakers that guide you into finding your ideal man or woman. However, there are general character traits that are basic in starting a relationship with the right foundation. When you fall in love, you are likely to bypass the flaws of your partner. Most of the time your friends or people outside of your relationship will see the flaws and alert you about it but you will overlook them. Maybe, confirmation that love is blind. You can achieve your relationship dreams, but if you don't take time to consider these qualities, you may miss your ideal partner.

Charitable: The first quality while looking at your ideal partner is being charitable. There are many things that will be needed in a relationship. However, a relationship is not one-sided and that means you will work as a team. Your ideal partner, however, should be able to offer unrestricted help when you are in need. This does not mean only financial help but also time spent with you, available to help with daily chores, charitable to the community and other family members. Being charitable and generous is inborn and cannot be forced. You also cannot say that you will help them be charitable after you start dating. This will not work because you cannot change a person unless they are willing to change. Being charitable is a virtue. You can check this with how he treats people in general.

Calmness: In each relationship, you aim to create a strong sustainable bond that brings peace of mind. No one wishes to have a dramatic love relationship. Choosing a chaotic partner will leave you emotionally exhausted. It is said that girls fall for bad boys while boys fall for dramatic queens. Well, when planning to get into a long-term relationship, you got to throw this notion over the window and welcome a calm human. Bad boys and drama queens will only give you heartbreaks and inconsistency. A calm partner will be consistent with their feelings towards you. A person who is not consistent will exhaust your physical and emotional being.

Willpower: A partner who does not have personal will power affects the drive of the other partner. Your ideal partner should be one with willpower to build their own successful path. Where there is will power, the relationship will take a healthy foundation. You have seen couples who have broken up because they set a wrong foundation. Love is important but also personal drive and determination is a necessity while building a relationship. It is important that your ideal partner has a motivation to provide a peaceful and successful life for both of you.

Compassion: It is important to seek a partner who is compassionate. This is someone who is sensitive to their surrounding environment. They recognize that you are human and respect your emotions. Your dreams of finding a soulmate will crush if you find an insensitive person. There are people who are cold and ignorant of your feelings. With them, you will always have to ask and remind them how to treat you and your needs. A soulmate will know what you need even before you ask them.

Personal development: It is said that you cannot give what you do not have. You give from a cup which is overflowing. This applies too when finding a partner. A person who does not treat themselves well, will not treat you well either. They should put their personal development as a priority. A partner who is always negative and speaks negatively about themselves will not make your dream come true. They will not lift you up but rather contribute to destroying you. A right partner should be able to prioritize their personal development in terms of lifestyle, inner person and their surroundings. It is then that they will be able to extend the same to you.

Dedication: Duty Enduring connections are the profoundly satisfying bonds we long for not sentiments that start and end too rapidly. You should probably rely upon somebody as long as possible; an accomplice who not just needs to preserve a relationship for a mind-blowing remainder, yet one who comprehends the exertion, bargain, and penance included. It is excessively easy to end up entrapped with an individual who stops when hard times arise. It's an indication of a perfect partner when you experience a person who communicates the craving for long-lasting duty and fortifies their words with activities.

Similarity: A relationship must be kept up if two individuals see the world with similar eyes. They should have similar objectives, thoughts, and outlook on what's to come. The association will self-destruct in the event that one individual needs to live in a condo without any kids, and the other needs to live in a major house with an enormous family. Two people should be open into coming together for a common decision about the basics of life. What is significant is that the two people keep on picturing a similar future, despite how each is gradually changing from the everyday.

There is no such thing as the ideal individual, however, there are sure components we should look for before engaging in romantic relationships for sustainability. Seek after affection as per these seven standards to experience an individual who may very well be your perfect partner.

Chapter Two

BOUNDARIES BEFORE CHOOSING A SOUL MATE

What to do before you enter into a relationship

Meeting a soulmate is one thing, and keeping the relationship blazing is another. Dating can be wearisome. Finding a soulmate can seem like a long quest. But there may be a good reason for it. According to experts, there are some hard lessons you need to learn before you get into a romantic relationship. Otherwise, you may hinder yourself from having a successful relationship. A lot of young people are in agreement that they are looking for a life partner who is also their soulmate. This is guided by a misconception of who is a soulmate. There is a notion that a soulmate is a person who is meant to be yours naturally without putting in any effort. When you have this thought, it is hard to find someone who can live upto it or rather, they cannot keep up forever.

Most of the time, romantic relationships end even before they begin. This is because of our own limitations. When you decide to engage in a romantic relationship, there are some things you need to work on in order to avoid relationship problems.

Look at Yourself: Before you commit to a person, you certainly need to investigate yourself. It's imperative to have total familiarity with your identity, your qualities, and shortcomings, before getting into a relationship. Take note of your identity. It is only in that that you will be able to know what you want in life.

Assess Your Religious Personality: Regardless of whether you are religious or not, this is something else you need to work through before getting into a relationship. For instance, a person raised in a Christian family may find it hard to marry an atheist or a Hindu who cannot marry a Muslim. Basically, you don't need a similar religion to make a relationship work, however the regard for one another's religion, or need thereof, ought to be there.

Leave the past: In the event that you've been scorched in past connections, it's significant not to contrast your present relationship with your past accomplices. It's not reasonable for you or to them. The one basic thing at the beginning of each new relationship is abandoning your past connections.

Timing and Desires: Obviously examining desires for yourself, your accomplice, and your relationship is significant, yet you likewise need to talk about your desires with respect to where you need to be in your relationship at one point. Some people have specific timelines in dating. Some meet, engage and marry in one year. Others take their time or have no interest in a long-term relationship. You coming into a relationship with a goal for marriage, while the other does not have a goal, then the relationship becomes shaky. It is important that you make it clear from the very beginning about your goals and intentions to avoid wasting time.

Pay attention to your partner: In spite of the fact that we're all equipped for tuning in, it's the capacity to genuinely hear somebody that is generally significant. Also, you need to really hear your accomplice before you get into an association with them. While there are no certifications throughout everyday life, in the event that you begin with a tough establishment and go from that point, you very well might have a superior shot at a fruitful relationship. In the event that you think about your relationship like a house, at that point it's obvious to perceive any reason why an establishment is so essential. You can't simply build a house, with nothing sufficient to hold it up and make it last.

Regardless of whether you feel like religion probably won't be an issue, in the end, it could be, so think about covering it now particularly on the off chance that you plan on having kids together sooner or later.

Setting Boundaries in a Relationship

There're a lot of misguided judgments about what limits are what they do for relationships. We may feel that boundaries are pointless because our partner should know and follow up on our needs, or that they ruin the relationship or meddle with the flavor. Truly, all solid connections have limits! A relationship can't be sound until the two convey their limits obviously, and the other individual regards them. Sound limits in a relationship won't fall into place easily, nor do they come effectively. The following is a rundown of both sound and undesirable viewpoints in a relationship:

Healthy	Unhealthy
Feeling in charge of your own happiness	Feeling imperfect without your partner
Companionships exist outside of the relationship	Relying on your partner for joy
Transparent communication	There is control
Tolerating endings	Unable to give up

Building up solid limits in a relationship enables the two to feel good and create positive confidence. So as to set up limits, you should be clear with your partner on your identity, what you need, your convictions and qualities, and your points of confinement. A ton of times, we will be pointing to other people, diverting from concentrating on ourselves. Defining limits for yourself that reflect your identity will just improve defining limits with your partner in a relationship.

Below are a few instances of boundaries.

- Your accomplice has plainly spoken with you that they don't need you to experience or utilize any of their assets except if you ask them first. You get in your vehicle to go to the mall, yet your vehicle won't start. Your partner is sleeping, so you promptly choose to utilize their vehicle.

- You've set a limit for yourself that you won't let anybody control what you do in a relationship, and you've discussed this limit with your partner. Later, they call you and asks what you have planned for the night, and you reveal to them you're going out with companions. Your accomplice discloses to you that you're not going, and in the event that they discover you did, there will be some sort of result. Due to that, you cancel your plans.

In the first example, your partner clearly stated that they don't want you using their stuff without their permission, but you disregarded your partner's limits by using their vehicle without consent. This could seem like a small thing to you, but it could be a big deal to your partner. In the second example, you have set a personal boundary of not allowing anyone to control you. Further, you disregarded it. That means you are not consistent with your own boundary.

If you are about to enter into a relationship with someone whom you fear, then that is a red flag. A person in a healthy relationship should not be afraid of their partner's reactions. Regardless of how big or small the boundary may be, it should be held up.

Here are a couple of tips to enable you to begin setting up limits with your partner in your relationship:

- *Communicate your considerations with each other.* Be straightforward, yet conscious when imparting your emotions to your partner. It's absolutely alright to need time to accumulate your musings and sentiments yet use that to create a distance from the discussion.
- *Making assumptions.* Making assumptions can make a great deal in a relationship. You may feel like you know

your partner such that you can assume what they do or need. However, it could be wrong and lead to disappointments. It is always advisable to discuss first.

- *Follow through on what you state.* Defining limits and not executing them gives the other individual a chance to think they have a reason to keep on violating your limits. You shouldn't make any special cases to your own limits without cautious though since you may end up trading off things that aren't satisfactory to you.

- *Take duty regarding your activities.* Rather than promptly censuring your partner for the circumstance, make a stride back and consider the decisions you've made in the relationship and check whether they may have added to the circumstance.

- *Know when it's a great opportunity to proceed onward.* You can just share how you want to be treated in the relationship, and you can't be in charge of your partner's emotions. Everybody has the privilege to be treated with deference and reasonableness. In the event that your partner can't regard your limits, at that point it might be an ideal opportunity to cut off the association.

Defining and building up solid limits is an ability, and it requires some serious energy. Keep in mind, solid limits don't come simple, however in the event that you heed your gut feelings, be open, and practice with your accomplice, the relationship will just get more grounded after some time.

Consciously choosing a partner

There's nothing more awful than getting profound into a relationship and after that abruptly understanding that you've settled on a poor decision. Before you get into a submitted association with another person, it's critical to maintain a strategic distance from a portion of the regular slip-ups.

Perhaps the greatest mix-up individuals make is turning into a "dopamine dope." In the beginning times of a relationship, a compound called dopamine is discharged in the mind that outcomes in a high. It lessens your capacity to think obviously and see your accomplice equitably.

Such many individuals center around establishing an incredible connection as opposed to remembering what they need, being consistent with themselves and getting a charge out of the present minute without forming a hasty opinion. By requiring some serious energy, you can become more acquainted with your accomplice and measure whether you have security and association.

Here is a Guide for Conscious Choices in a Partner.

Graciousness and Respect: The articulation, "we should treat family like outsiders and outsiders like family," is characteristic of the measure of lack of regard that is endured seeing someone. This disposition is a boundary to the fundamental structure squares of long-haul generosity and regard.

Capacity to Learn: Curiosity: Although it is entirely expected to have differences and power battles, numerous couples neglect to gain from clashes and may rehash similar reckless situations and practices for quite a long time. We shouldn't talk except if we can enhance quietness. As James Thurber noticed, our propensity is to think back in indignation or forward in dread, rather than "around in mindfulness."

Adaptability: Many individuals experienced childhood in inflexible families, with unbending jobs. Thusly, it doesn't jump out at them to relinquish designs that unmistakably aren't working.

Capacity to Hear Your Pain: This is the thing that frequently brings couples into treatment since they have not figured out how to sit and hear one out another with sympathy and empathy.

A Deep Inner Life on A Personal Journey: Often couples turns out to be also melded, losing their individual delights and interests.

Comparative Passions: Many couples lose their pleasure bond with one another, sharing for the most part grumblings and toiler.

Comparative Values: Unfortunately, we read too much "joyfully ever after" fantasies, rather than understanding the significance of the cognizant arrangement of standards, jobs, religion, and cash issues, right off the bat in couple-hood.

Sympathy: Many individuals learn "disgrace and fault" games in their family. They take part in blackguard chasing and figure out how to utilize these practices in cozy connections. Families neglect to observe each other with "delicate eyes," (Levine 1995) so as to address issue practices in a delicate way without judgment about toward accomplices. Frequently an accomplice will take the "ethical high ground" and talk to the next about saw insufficiencies. Rather, of empathy shared between two equivalents, accomplices regularly identify with one another like they are guardians of kids.

Capacity to Laugh at One's Self. Because numerous individuals experienced childhood in a disgrace accuses condition, it is hard for them to take a gander at themselves delicately.

Substance Abuse, Dishonesty, Cover-up. An absence of information about substance misuse brings a special case into connections. Additionally, deceitfulness and conceal cause development of terrible sentiments, getting to be "dark-colored stamps." This can prompt what I call the "anchovy pizza" disorder. In my training, I have seen incalculable couples who've spared "dark-colored stamps" of awful emotions until they are prepared to trade them out at the separation reclamation focus. In one such case, a lady spared book after book of terrible sentiments about her significant other's failure to hear her needs. The last stamp was glued when he requested an anchovy pizza. She detested anchovies. At that point, she reported, to his stun, that the pizza was the last nourishment he'd ever request for her since she needed separation.

Capacity to Be A Friend and Not Just A Lover: Passion without fellowship seeing someone, resembles doing somersaults on a carnival trapeze without a security net.

Somebody Who Makes Your Life Bigger, Not Smaller. Unfortunately, an excessive number of individuals grew up observing family as far as remedy city, menial worker and obligation. Subsequently, they see responsibility as a jail sentence, rather than a mutual experience.

Even though this is a simple rundown to retain, the trouble lays in breaking the examples that anticipate upkeep of our ideal practices. Peggy Papp, a well-known family specialist commented that we leave our own group of starting point with a "cutout" way to deal with life and it requires "gallant minutes" to change the state of our own dough shapers.

Envision your fantasy relationship a few times each day and that will start to change your cutout. Concentrate on who and what you need, rather than who and what you don't need. Just a single individual can vanquish you in the undertaking, that individual is you. Inward redress makes external rectification.

When to leave a relationship

In the event that good-natured and minding individuals can, without blame or fault, perceive the manifestations that disclose to them that they have to give up, they can cut off their association without disdain or sentiments of sat around idly. On the off chance that couples remain excessively long in a relationship that can't beat that, they hazard losing the chance to love the exercises they have adapted together.

Here are the eleven most basic indications that messenger a relationship that is probably going to end:

Little Irritations That Grate Over Time

Each new relationship has both great associations and not all those great ones. New darlings do their best to value the normally fulfilling associations and overlook those that are bothering. Shockingly, after some time, a portion of the distressful practices start to putrefy and are more diligently for the other accomplice to disregard. They can be seemingly insignificant details like leaving garments on the floor, being constantly late, or overlooking a guarantee.

There are additionally increasingly genuine ones like as yet remaining nearby to an old kid or young lady companion, getting excessively alcoholic, or not paying bills on schedule. At the point when these disquieting practices hit a minimum amount, the other accomplice might be not able to endure them any longer.

At the point when the great associations are disintegrated by gathered feelings of hatred, the relationship's equalization moves off course, and the decency that once kept the organization unblemished moves toward becoming covered under layers of dissatisfaction and thwarted expectation.

Unsatisfactory Behaviors That Were Not Revealed toward the Beginning of the Relationship

Most new darlings intentionally cover up past practices that have contrarily influenced their different connections. They trust that, when the new relationship is built up, their accomplice will be bound to pardon those old offenses.

Regardless of how tolerant another accomplice might be, there are additionally sure late admissions that can devastate even the most alluring of connections. The accomplice who has gotten tied up with accepting that the other is dependable in those urgent regions might be not able to acknowledge past practices that challenge both that they occurred at all and that they were disguised in any case.

Here are some regular models:

Enormous obligations that must be inevitably paid out of common assets

An unmentioned youngster

Past affiliations with not exactly alluring characters who may manifest once more

An earlier marriage

An inheritable infection

Meddling and controlling guardian sneaking out of sight

Any past shrouded conduct that may be unsatisfactory to another accomplice can be a major issue when it is at long last uncovered. Regardless of whether one accomplice should educate another concerning them can fluctuate by the earnestness of the issue and whether its consequence will at last influence the new relationship.

These normal models can be difficult to suffer, and it is up to every individual when to share them. There are additionally intense issues that must be shared in advance, even though the hazard is high. For example, if a potential accomplice has an STD that could undermine wellbeing, a noxious ex or spouse, or an earlier lawful offense conviction that may influence what's to come.

Fundamentally unrelated Important Needs

When minding accomplices are first together, they emphasize the manners in which they can love one another, consider contrasts, and attempt to drive away so far unrevealed needs with the expectation that the extending love between them will at last purpose the circumstance.

Unfortunately, a few accomplices find after some time that they can't live with certain essentially significant various needs or wants. Probably the most well-known are diverse sexual hunger, different dreams, or how to manage earlier accomplices, however, there are numerous others. By what method should our cash be designated? What is our optimal spot to live? What several kids, assuming any, would it be a good idea for us to have? Do we deal with our folks? What are our criteria for companionships? What amount of time away from one another would we be able to endure? How would we impart, and would we be able to determine significant clashes?

These potential contrasts occasionally become known right off the bat in a relationship. It is just when assets are pooled that accomplices start to uncover what they can live without, bargain on, or are reluctant to change. Those distinctions should be dealt with common regard and backing, yet regularly bring out practices that neither one of the partners could have foreseen, nor can live with.

Reducing Illusions

Goodness, the visual impairment of new love. The accomplices who relish those early minutes will hang on beyond a reasonable doubt to the delight of their euphoria. They endeavor to ignore blemishes and decorate those characteristics that make their new accomplice greater than life.

It is typical for those overstated hallucinations to decrease after some time and the accomplices develop to know each other more profoundly. What is considered exceedingly alluring toward the start may have a negative drawback that isn't uncovered until the relationship develops? For example, an accomplice committed to his or her main purpose for existing may appear to be sublimely great, however then disillusions that accomplice by time after time organizing that dedication over the relationship. An extremely appealing accomplice who commits a lot of time keeping up that outcome may appear to be too self-intrigued. An individual superbly cautious about not overspending can, after some time, seem miserly and shabby. An energetic accomplice who is at first exceptionally sexual might be substantially less so as different needs develop.

An individual who guarantees less and conveys more can be a delight, yet it's an uncommon quality. New sweethearts don't for the most part center around potential frustrations. At the point when things calm down, the accomplices are in line to make new evaluations of what is great, what requirements improvement, and what might be unsatisfactory.

Outer Stressors

The synergistic vitality of another relationship seems vast. The couple's association makes more than the whole of the parts. Bottomless in the vitality to face a challenge, they believe they can confront any emergency, sudden or foreseen.

Tragically, assets are not perpetual, and an excessive number of stressors can disintegrate the most profound of duties. Real diseases, mishaps, work requests, loss of money related soundness, family needs, sorrow over misfortune, or a progression of wild disillusionments can erode at a couple's capacity to adapt. On the off chance that those stressors proceed, they may lose confidence in the relationship's ability to endure them.

Stressors extend a couple's ability to learn and develop. On the off chance that they can't triumph over them, they risk finding each other insufficient. Criticizing each other's responses and reactions, they will start to lose trust and separate to tackle their issues alone. Here and there is simply an excessive amount of anguish, and any relationship can go down when a lot of is excessive.

Power Struggles

At the point when love is new, the two accomplices are happy to settle. They settle on choices together, verifying each other's conclusions and making progress toward understanding. Sharing the ability to decide, they become an incorporated group making commonly settled upon arrangements.

As the relationship develops, either accomplice may express his or her wants, predispositions, and preferences with greater force. Over and over again, this procedure brings about corresponding preventiveness with the two accomplices may turn to shield their positions and attempting to weight the other into consenting.

What may have been a common choice to get to know each other may turn into an issue if one accomplice needs additional time alone and different needs to impart that opportunity to other people. For instance, the more social accomplice may now need to carry different companions into the relationship or invest energy away without the other accomplice. Maybe one accomplice needs tranquil, separate time, leaving the other inclination desolate and deserted. Either may have utilized sweet enticement, delicate intimidation, or welcome before, however, now has become annoyed and utilizes progressively exceptional influences. Maybe either may compromise outcomes that are, as a rule, shrouded strategic maneuvers for control. Harmful battles supplant past trade-offs as each competes to win.

Power battles can bring about accomplices simply leaving, fuming in outrage, making edgy supplications, or utilizing blame as a beating stick. They may not understand they are carrying on that way, yet plainly what appears as though a guiltless welcome has now turned into an interest with a reasonable "or the consequences will be severe" behind it.

On the off chance that power battles endure, couples go from being a group to enemies on inverse sides of the playing field. Too early, they start to spare themselves to the detriment of different needs.

Getting to be shallow

It is difficult for anybody to be valid and open in another relationship. Keeping things light, surface, and non-compromising is progressively basic conduct. Be that as it may, as adoration develops, effective couples start to extend their correspondence and go out on a limb in sharing their vulnerabilities and blemishes. They are happy to be known in increasingly helpless ways and to listen all the more profoundly to one another. That lavishness of profundity in correspondence and sharing turns into the couple's mark of affection.

It is very normal and horribly tragic when accomplices can't go past shallow associations. Without the fearlessness or capacity to enable their center selves to associate, the relationship will fall prey to shallow associations after some time.

There are numerous reasons why darlings are reluctant to associate at a more profound level. Weakness can make them apprehensive that their accomplices will love them less if they know excessively. Maybe, when they've attempted before, they have had terrible encounters and felt dismissal, deserting, or negation.

On the off chance that they've attempted in their present relationship and not been generally welcomed, they may have drawn back and come back to acting in manners that appear to be less compromising. As cozy discussions become increasingly troublesome, a couple's shot of sharing essences in an extending path starts to terminate. Before long, they are bound to share who they truly are with others, instead of with one another. Dreadful of scarring the relationship further, they remain with agreeable and non-undermining words and practices.

After some time, their communications become unsurprising customs, requiring less and less exertion. To other people, they may seem, by all accounts, to be perfect, however, they are extremely simply rehashing known and secure ongoing practices. In time they will end up helpless to new and progressively charming encounters.

Weariness

Steady disclosure of the other accomplice's interior and outside changes is the establishment of dependable, developing connections. Since accomplices in new connections are generally "all that could possibly be needed" to fulfill one another, they frequently don't understand that their very own autonomous development is a fundamental prerequisite for remaining in adoration.

If two or three has bent over backward to know each other profoundly and reaches the finish of that disclosure, they will start to underestimate one another and put less vitality into a dull and routine relationship. Taking the situation of "aren't I adequate as I am," or "You knew my identity when we met and it was alright at that point, wasn't it?" are justifications that spread the absence of enthusiasm for nonstop development.

All the time one accomplice pushes forward in his or her advancement and the other enduringly remains the equivalent. On the off chance that no measure of solicitations, arguing, or compromising changes that design, the individual who was once excited will feel entangled in same-old-same-old, and requirements to proceed onward.

Deadness

Connections have two noteworthy measurements, developing and scarring. In the event that a relationship continually scars and doesn't develop, the passionate scarring will inevitably swarm the relationship and crush it. On the off chance that the relationship the two scars regularly, however, keeps on developing, it will be always in transition, with accomplices who shift back and forth among harming and recuperating. These connections regularly proceed for significant lots of time however for the most part, in the end, exhaust the accomplices who are in them. At the point when a relationship only from time to time scars and is in steady change, the accomplices inside it are fortunate individuals who will presumably never lose enthusiasm for one another.

The last conceivable blend is a relationship that neither scars nor develops. Superficially, it might appear a mysteriously perfect, discreetly fruitful association, however, the absence of fervor and vitality watched can be an amazing cautioning sign that there is inconvenience blending. The accomplices inside it might have turned out to be automated and unsurprising animals who before long become familiar with one another's each expression, activity, and thought. They never again need to give much consideration to recognize what is happening. There are no curveballs, no difficulties, and no development.

These individuals appear to experience life as though in a place of mirrors. For whatever length of time that there is no contention, they don't shade outside the lines nor feel their vitality lessening. On the off chance that their detached conduct is kept to the relationship, they will, in the long run, want to sit quietly to one another, and even decreased energy. On the off chance that they are getting their requirements for a change somewhere else, the inconsistency between their conduct inside and outside of the relationship will, in the long run, eradicate either.

Self-Serving Escapes That Become More Important Than the Primary Relationship

Addictions are the most outstanding models. Addictive practices are just impulsive, critical guilty pleasures that remove one accomplice from the other and cause long haul harm to a private relationship. Regardless of whether medications and liquor, social commitment, contribution in games or body wellness, or intemperate work duties, they are contending connections that take a point of reference over the essential one, and channel its vitality. An accomplice on the opposite finish of an addictive mate isn't given a vote to keep the essential relationship unblemished. Just the accomplice who takes part in the addictive conduct can settle on the choice to re-organize the vitality that the person is spending somewhere else.

The triangles between two submitted individuals when one is dependent on something, or somebody, else will consistently decrease the one of a kind bonds between them. At whatever point a person or thing turns out to be more critical to one accomplice than to the next, the relationship will be compromised. On the off chance that the addictive accomplice isn't eager to take a gander at the expense of his or her choice, the accomplice denied of a vote will, in the long run, become upset enough to detach.

Any break that contends, reduces or compromises a relationship ought to be reasonable play for investigation and fix. Keep in mind, the basic assets of a relationship must be dispersed by a common understanding of the organization is imperative to both. One individual can't singularly choose to utilize those assets without the authorization of the other without devastating the sacredness of that understanding.

Raising Misunderstandings and Misassumptions

Numerous individuals in developing connections overlook how to listen cautiously without making a hasty judgment, particularly concerning what their accomplices are really feeling or thinking. They accept that commonality has qualified them for supposing they know it all they have to about the other, regardless of whether either has changed.

Life's difficulties can take individuals' vitality away from their relationship and put its investigation on a back burner. All the time after some time, the accomplices accept they never again need to try to reestablish their enthusiasm for new needs. They keep making presumptions dependent on old or erroneous information and miss pivotal changes and implications that could adjust their reactions.

Before long, the couple's correspondence comprises of brief expressions and mistaken suspicions. They lose enthusiasm for one another and neglect to determine mistaken assumptions. As these damaging cooperation's duplicate, the accomplices may never again attempt to unravel the wreckage and let the layers of overlooked passionate garbage amass.

Chapter Three

DECISIONS THAT INFLUENCE THE CHOICE OF A SOUL MATE

Disappointed single individuals ought to really think about themselves in a nonpartisan, genuinely cheerful position, contrasted with what their circumstance could be. A solitary individual who might want to locate an incredible relationship is one stage away from it, with their daily agenda perusing to find an extraordinary relationship. People in troubled connections, then again, are three jumps away, with a plan for the day of; going through a spirit squashing separation and emotional recoup. Not as terrible when you take a gander at it that way, correct? All the examination on how immensely bliss changes among glad and miserable relationships comprehends, course. It's your life accomplice.

Contemplating how overwhelmingly significant it is to pick the correct life accomplice resembles pondering how enormous the universe truly is or how frightening demise truly is—it's too extreme to even consider internalizing its truth, so we simply don't consider it that hard and stay in slight refusal about the extent of the circumstance. Yet, in contrast to the death and the universe's size, picking a soulmate is completely in your control, so it's basic to make yourself totally clear on how enormous an arrangement the choice truly is and to altogether dissect the most significant factors in making it.

So how enormous of an arrangement is it?

Indeed, begin by subtracting your age from 90. In the event that you carry on with long life, that is about the number of years you will go through with your present or future life accomplice, plus or minus a couple. Without a doubt, individuals get separated, yet you don't figure you will. An ongoing report demonstrates that 86% of youngsters expect their present or future marriage will be perpetually, and I question more established individuals feel much in an unexpected way. So, we'll continue under that supposition. What's more, when you pick an actual life partner, you're picking a great deal of things, including your child-rearing accomplice and somebody who will profoundly impact your kids, you're eating partner for around 20,000 dinners, your movement friend for around 100 excursions, your essential relaxation time and retirement companion, your profession advisor, and somebody whose day you'll find out about multiple times. So, given this is by a wide margin the most significant thing in life to get right, how is it conceivable that such a significant number of good, savvy, generally intelligent individuals wind up picking partners that leave them disappointed? There are a lot of variables including:

Individuals will, in general, be terrible at recognizing what they need from a relationship: Studies have indicated individuals to be commonly awful, when single, at foreseeing what later end up being their real relationship inclinations. One examination found that speed daters interrogated regarding their relationship inclinations normally substantiate themselves wrong only minutes after the fact with what they show to lean toward in the genuine occasion. This shouldn't be a shock—throughout everyday life, you normally don't get the hang of something until you've done it a lot of times. Lamentably, relatively few individuals get an opportunity to be in excess of a barely any, genuine connections before they settle on their major choice. There's sufficiently not time. What's more, given that an individual's organization persona and relationship needs are frequently very not quite the same as the manner in which they are as a solitary individual, it's hard as a solitary individual to truly recognize what you need or need from a relationship.

Society has everything incorrectly and offers us horrendous guidance

Society urges us to remain uneducated and let sentiment be our guide.

In case you're maintaining a business, the customary way of thinking states that you're a substantially more powerful entrepreneur on the off chance that you study business in school, make all-around idea out marketable strategies, and dissect your business' exhibition tirelessly. This is intelligent, on the grounds that that is the way you continue when you need to accomplish something admirably and limit botches. In the event that somebody went to class to find out about how to pick an actual existence accomplice and partake in a solid relationship, in the event that they graphed an itemized strategy to discover one, and in the event that they kept their advancement sorted out thoroughly in a spreadsheet, society says they are, an over-sound robot. No, with regards to dating, society disapproves of reasoning a lot about it, rather choosing things like depending on destiny, going with your gut, and seeking after the best. In the event that an entrepreneur accepted society's dating guidance for her business, she'd most likely come up short, and on the off chance that she succeeded, it would be in part because of good karma and that is the manner by which society needs us to approach dating.

Society puts a shame on raising our standards for potential partners.

In an investigation on what administers our dating decisions more, our inclinations or our present chances, openings win pass on our dating decisions are "98% a reaction… to economic situations and just 2% unchanging wants. The proposition to date tall, short, fat, slight, proficient, administrative, taught, uneducated individuals, are on the whole more than nine-tenths represented by what's on offer that night."

At the end of the day, individuals wind up picking from whatever pool of choices they have, regardless of how ineffectively coordinated they may be to those up-and-comers. The undeniable determination to make here is that outside of genuine socialites, everybody searching for an actual existence accomplice ought to complete a ton of web-based dating, speed dating, and different frameworks made to expand the up-and-comer pool in an insightful manner.

However, great old society disapproves of that, and individuals are frequently still shy to state they met their life partner on a dating site. The decent method to meet a real existence accomplice is by blind luckiness, by finding them haphazardly or being acquainted with them from inside your little pool. Luckily, this disgrace is lessening with time, yet that it's there at all is an impression of how nonsensical the socially acknowledged dating rulebook is.

Society hurries us: In our reality, the significant principle is to get hitched before you're excessively old—and "excessively old" differs from 25 – 35, contingent upon where you live. The standard ought to be "whatever you do, don't wed an inappropriate individual," however society glares substantially more upon a 37-year-old single individual than it looks at an unhealthy 37-year-old marriage. It has neither rhyme nor reason the previous is one stage away from a cheerful marriage, while the last should either agree to perpetual despondency or persevere through a muddled separation just to make up for lost time.

Our science is doing us no favors: Human science advanced quite a while prior and doesn't comprehend the idea of having a profound association with a real existence accomplice for a long time. When we begin seeing somebody and feel the smallest twinge of fervor, our science gets into an agreement mode and shells us with synthetics intended to get us to mate experience passionate feelings, and after that submit for the long run connection. Our minds can ordinarily abrogate this procedure in case we're simply not that into somebody, however, for every one of those center ground situations where the correct move is presumably to proceed onward and discover something better, we regularly capitulate to the concoction crazy ride and wind up getting ready for marriage.

Natural timekeepers: For a lady who needs to have kids with her significant other, she has one genuine confinement in play, which is the need to pick the correct life accomplice by forty years. This is only a crappy certainty and makes an officially hard procedure one score progressively distressing. In any case, on the off chance that it was me, I'd preferably adopt kids with the correct life accomplice over have natural kids with an inappropriate one. So, when you take a lot of individuals who aren't that great at knowing what they need in a relationship, encompass them with a general public that discloses to them they need to discover an actual existence accomplice yet that they ought to under think, under investigate and hustle just a bit. A free for all of the significant choices for terrible reasons and many individuals wrecking the most significant choice of their life. How about we investigate a portion of the basic sorts of individuals who succumb to the majority of this and cut off up in troubled associations:

Romance: Romantic emotions can be an incredible piece of a relationship, and love is a key fixing in a glad marriage, however without a lot of other significant things, it's essentially insufficient. The excessively sentimental individual more than once overlooks the little voice that attempts to talk up when he and his better half are battling always or when he appears to feel much more awful about himself nowadays than he used to before the relationship, closing the voice down with musings like "Everything occurs for a reason and the manner in which we met couldn't have quite recently been incident" and "I'm absolutely enamored with her, and that is the only thing that is important"— when an excessively sentimental individual accepts he's discovered his perfect partner, he quits addressing things, and he'll cling to that conviction entirely through his 50 years of miserable marriage.

Panic: Panic is one of the most exceedingly terrible conceivable things with regards to picking the correct life partner. Tragically, the way society is set up, panic begins contaminating a wide range of something else levelheaded individuals, at times as ahead of schedule as the mid-twenties. The kinds of dread our general public (and guardians, and companions) perpetrate upon us dread of being the last single companion, the dread of being a more established parent, once in a while simply dread of being judged or discussed—are the sorts that lead us to agree to a not very good organization. The incongruity is that the main sound dread we should feel is the dread of spending the last 66% of life miserably, with an inappropriate individual—the definite destiny the dread driven individual's hazard since they're attempting to be chance opposed.

Pressure from outside: Pressure gives other individuals a chance to have too huge an influence on the choice of a partner. The picking of an actual existence accomplice is profoundly close to home, immensely entangled, distinctive for everybody, and practically difficult to comprehend all things considered, regardless of how well you know somebody. Accordingly, other individuals' assessments and inclinations truly have no spot getting included, other than an outrageous case including abuse or misuse. The saddest case of this is somebody saying a final farewell to an individual who might have been the correct life person due to outside objection or a factor the chooser doesn't really think about i.e. religion, however, feels constrained to adhere to for family request or desires. It can likewise happen the contrary way, where everybody in somebody's life is excited with his relationship since it looks incredible all things considered, and despite the fact that it's not really that extraordinary from within, Ed tunes in to others over his very own gut and gets married.

Physical qualities: You may be increasingly worried about the on-paper depiction of your partner than the inward character underneath it. There are a lot of boxes that she needs checked things like his tallness, work renown, riches level, achievements, or perhaps a knick-knack like being outside or having a particular ability. Everybody has sure on-paper boxes they'd like checked; however, an unequivocal sense of self-driven individual organizes appearances and list of references above even the nature of her association with her potential life accomplice when gauging things. On the off chance that you need a fun new term, a critical other whom you think was picked more on account of the cases they checked than for their character underneath is an examine tron sweetheart or since they effectively round out every one of the air pockets. I've gotten some great mileage out of that one.

Jealousy: This individual can't deal with penance or bargain. They trust their needs and wants, and assessments are basically more significant than their partner's, and she needs to get her way in practically any critical choice. At last, she doesn't need a real association, she needs to keep her single life and have somebody there to stay with her. This individual unavoidably winds up with, best case scenario a very accommodating individual, and even from a pessimistic standpoint, a weakling with a confidence issue, and forfeits an opportunity to be a piece of a group of equivalents, likely restricting the potential nature of her marriage.

The primary character

The Main Character's appalling defect is by and large enormously self-consumed. He needs a real existence accomplice who fills in as the two his specialist and greatest admirer yet is for the most part uninterested in returning either support. Every night, he and his accomplice talk about their days, yet 90% of the exchange bases on his day—all things considered, he's the primary character of the relationship. The issue for him is that by being unequipped for tearing himself away from his own reality, he winds up with a sidekick as his life accomplice, which makes for a truly exhausting 50 years.

The requirements driven

Everybody has requirements, and everybody prefers those should be met, yet issues emerge when the gathering of necessities—she cooks for me, he'll be an incredible dad, she'll make an extraordinary spouse, he's rich, she keeps me sorted out, he's incredible in bed—turns into the fundamental justification for picking somebody as an actual existence accomplice. Those recorded things are largely incredible advantages, however that is all they are—advantages. Furthermore, following a time of marriage, when the necessities driven individual is presently completely acquainted with having her needs met and it's never again energizing, there should be much progressively great pieces of the relationship she's picked or she's in for a dull ride.

The primary reason most of the above kinds cut off up in troubled associations is that they're devoured by a rousing power that doesn't consider the truth of what an actual existence organization is and what makes it a cheerful thing.

Choosing the right partner

Discover somebody who you can interface with effectively: It is critical to pick someone who you can undoubtedly hit a discussion with. Along these lines, you can appreciate getting things done and discussing them together without getting exhausted.

Similarity: Choosing somebody who offers a ton of normal interests with you will work to support you. Keep in mind that every one of your interests don't generally need to be the equivalent, yet some would do. When you choose to go through your time on earth with somebody, you should take a gander at things that you two couldn't imagine anything better than to do together.

Think about your accomplice's intelligence: If you are a laid-back individual and your accomplice is an over-achiever, that could prompt a risk in your marriage. You should agree on how both of you can think and process things.

It's alright to have measures: While picking an ideal partner, you have to consider your and your family's stand. In spite of the fact that it's alright to pick somebody who most likely does not have a place with indistinguishable strata of society from yours, ensure that he/she's not totally off the imprint.

You ought to have regard for each other: You clearly can't go through your time on earth with somebody who has no regard for you or your fantasies/objectives or your character. In this way, pick somebody who will recognize you for a mind-blowing remainder.

Is your potential dependable: These days, it is critical to pick somebody you can count on. You unquestionably can't lead an upbeat marriage on the off chance that you can't confide in one another or have confidence.

Get to know each other: Similarly, as significant all things considered to have comparable interests, it is additionally critical to be with somebody who gives you sufficient opportunity and who you couldn't imagine anything better than to invest energy with.

There's nothing more regrettable than getting profound into a relationship and afterward suddenly understanding that you've settled on a poor decision. Before you get into a submitted association with another person, it's imperative to maintain a strategic distance from a portion of the regular missteps.

Perhaps the greatest mix-up individuals make is turning into a "dopamine dope." In the beginning periods of a relationship a synthetic called dopamine is discharged in the cerebrum that outcomes in a high. It lessens your capacity to think unmistakably and see your accomplice dispassionately.

An excessive number of individuals center around establishing an extraordinary connection as opposed to remembering what they need, being consistent with themselves and getting a charge out of the present minute without making a hasty judgment. By requiring some investment, you can become more acquainted with your accomplice and measure whether you have wellbeing and association.

Chapter Four

WHAT COMPLICATES A RELATIONSHIP BEFORE IT BECOMES OFFICIAL?

Before you start dating

When you find your ideal partner, you will not jump in without carrying some rules. Here is what you should know;

Take as much time as necessary. Microwave connections don't take as much time or exertion; however, they are a weak, soaked, stale substitute for the genuine article.

Try not to say the "l-word"… yet! You can't profoundly cherish somebody on the off chance that you don't have any acquaintance with them. Butterflies can move around your stomach, melodies can latch onto your subconscious mind, yet on the off chance that you don't have a clue about an individual, you are essentially charmed by their anticipated self. Until you see their actual self and choose to remain, maintain a strategic distance from announcements of adoration.

Watch for notice signs. On the off chance that your relationship has more warnings than a Spanish bullfight, receive in return. Try not to convince yourself to remain. For instance, individuals who really regard and respect others will keep their pledge. Be with somebody who is thoughtful, reliable, mindful, fair, and certain.

Pay attention. The object of your love will be the subject of your observer. Individuals talk about what they're amped up for. Be with somebody who is amped up for Jesus. Watch their association with God develop and perceive how they bolster you in yours.

Know their consistent character. On the chance that I did it for you, I'll do it to you. If they went behind someone's back with you, they'll most likely go behind your back with another person.

Assemble your kinships. Solid connections develop with regards to network. In the event that a companion reveals to you that you are settling, and you don't have authentic motivations to refute them, that companion is correct. Hear them out. Try not to grow a relationship in obscurity. Let the light of your locale into that space.

Try not to represent externalization. You're more than your body. Thus, on the off chance that somebody treats you like a sex toy, let them go.

Keep away from untimely marriage discussions. When somebody says, "God disclosed to me we should get hitched" or something like that, and you don't feel a resonating YES! in your heart, be amazingly mindful of how you continue in the relationship. In the wake of picking Christ, the decision of your marriage accomplice is the most significant choice you will ever make. On the off chance that you haven't seen their character all through the periods of your relationship, those incredibly passionate discussions extend your relationship to an undesirable level.

Get help! Everybody has stuff, and everybody needs a little assistance in some cases. Be eager to go to treatment. Discover a guide or a holistic mentor. Peruse books that will support development. Your sound connections require your wellbeing. Make it a need and watch your whole world change.

When you get into a relationship, it can feel like occasions moves at twist speed. One minute you're simply dating, and the following you've been as one for a considerable length of time. Since things can occur so rapidly, it's imperative to truly realize yourself before beginning a relationship, in case you get cleared up in the hurricane, all things considered, and forget about yourself and your objectives.

But at the same time, it's essential to enter an organization in general, balanced individual as somebody who can add to the wellbeing of the relationship — on the grounds that life's currently about you two. You'll need to know how you best impart, what your shortcomings may be, how you intend to deal with funds, how you'll bargain the rundown continues endlessly.

When you know these things about yourself preceding getting in a relationship, they will enable you to have a more beneficial relationship and help you speak with your accomplice before issues emerge. Realizing yourself will likewise keep you on track to getting precisely what you need and need from your accomplice, while additionally sparing you from stalling out in something poisonous. Beneath, a couple of significant things you should know and consider before beginning another relationship.

Things that can push your partner away

There are things that will pose a challenge to your relationship before it materializes.

Not getting over your ex: Starting a new relationship before you get over the previous one will kill your dream of getting a soul mate. It is tough transitioning from a breakup. You are still filled with emotions and trying to get over it. Getting into another romantic relationship before you are emotionally ready to move for wad is a complication. You will find yourself trying to make your partner fill the gap of healing you while it is your own obligation to ensure that you are emotionally ready to move forward. A breakup makes you feel duped and wasted especially if long-term discussions and sex was involved. Therefore, before engaging in a new relationship, it is advisable that you get over your ex. Ensure you are ready for the next move. Emotional overlapping does not last long.

Cold treatment: There are challenges in each relationship. Sometimes, people may use silent treatment instead of communicating. This will not lead you to a long-term romantic relationship but rather, it will end it before it begins. Being silent on your ideal partner makes it hard to know each other. It's also hard to find solutions that can save the union.

Assuming your partner knows everything: It is wrong to assume that your partner knows everything that you need. You have seen women get dramatic after their boyfriend forgets that important date, or a thing they were to do together. Your partner cannot read your mind, it's important to communicate your needs articulately. Assumption may bring disappointments since your expectation is not met. This is because, not everyone is able to read minds and you may judge them wrongly. In a healthy relationship, you are supposed to be open to each other and to speak your mind without fear of judgement.

Victimization: You may have a challenge in your relationship. Following the right channel in solving the problem is important. However, you should not victimize your partner making them feel guilty. This has made many relationships fall even before they become something. I know woman whose husband had an affair, after realizing this, she played the guilt card for a whole year. This made it hard for them to heal their marriage and it was in the verge of collapsing before they decided to see a counselor. It is important to note that, trying to dig the past mistakes and victimizing your partner will draw you away from them. This will in turn kill your dreams of finding a soul mate.

Being resentful: Hushing up about your sentiments can appear to be simpler than communicating them when you're seeing someone. Sexologist and relationship masters reveal that doing as such could truly hurt your relationship. Nearly everybody knows about the circumstance when there is some strain and one partner inquire as to whether they are disturbed and the accomplice answers, 'I'm fine', yet things are without a doubt not fine. In any chance that you are vexed, the best activity is to say so. When you restrain your feelings, you can begin to develop feelings of disdain towards your partner. Those can putrefy and bring about a gigantic explode that could have been dodged if you simply tended to the worry from the earliest starting point. Your accomplice isn't a mind reader, so in any chance that they ask you, answer genuinely and talk candidly about it.

Conversations that are necessary before getting into a romantic relationship

Sex: Indeed, even partners who cherish each other can have sexual problems. Absence of sexual mindfulness and training intensifies these issues. In any case, engaging in sexual relations is one of the last things you should surrender, since it unites you, discharges hormones that help your bodies physically, and keeps the science of a solid couple sound. It is important to discuss these, issue at the beginning. It will help know where you both stand in regard to sexual matters. Do you want to have sex immediately or wait till engagement or marriage? I have seen many relationships that partners felt wasted after a romantic escapade because they were not on the same page in regard to where the relationship is heading.

Money: Money has broken many relationships. It is important that you discuss financial matters early in the relationship. Speak the truth about your current money related circumstance. In the event that things have gone south, proceeding with a similar way of life is unreasonable. Try not to approach the subject in the warmth of fight. Rather, put aside a period that is helpful and non-compromising for both of you. Recognize that one accomplice might be a saver and one a high roller, comprehend there are advantages to both, and consent to gain from one another's propensities. Try not to conceal salary or obligation. Bring monetary records, including an ongoing credit report, and ventures to the table. Choose which individual will oversee paying the month to month bills. Enable every individual to have autonomy by putting aside cash to be spent at his or her tact. Settle on present moment and long-haul objectives. It's OK to have singular objectives, yet you ought to have family objectives, as well. Discussion about thinking about your folks as they age and how to properly get ready for their money related needs if necessary.

Disagreement: Occasional conflict is a part of life. It is good to speak your mind and find out what makes you angry and what each of you does to resolve it. If you do not discuss how to solve disagreements together, it will crush your relationship. Lessen the anger and make strategic ways in which you will be resolving it together. You can argue in a modest manner, without blame game. Be truthful to yourself and think before jumping into conclusions.

Reliance: Being reliable is key in a relationship. It means that you can be trusted. It is important that you discuss issues around trust and the fears that each individual comes with into the relationship. To build trust, it will be important to hold certain values that can work. Heed to your promise. Keep time, always tell the truth, and be sensitive to your partners' feelings.

(Dear reader, if the way we are dealing with this theme is of interest to you, leave us your review on Amazon, for us it is important...)

Unhealthy relationship

Connections are something we have from the minute we are conceived until we kick the bucket. Sound or undesirable, our connections start with our folks, families, classmates, companions, etc. All these connections can enable us, to advance us, and improve us individuals just as basically give us happiness. Unfortunate connections occasionally advance any of these emotions. Undesirable connections can leave us feeling awkward, pitiful and apprehensive. It is exceptionally hard for individuals to give the acknowledgment a chance to set in that maybe a companion, colleague or relative isn't treating them well or aware, as they ought to be. It very well may be significantly increasingly troublesome when the individual treating them along these lines is a darling.

This doesn't mean if somebody treats you severely or you have a contradiction that the relationship is naturally undesirable. Contradictions occur in solid connections constantly. Frequently what makes a relationship sound is the need and the demonstration of bargaining when differences happen.

Control and Abuse: The unfortunate relationship is defaced by a need to control either. At the point when contentions occur, an individual is constantly made to feel awful about themselves; when criticism and ridiculing is the standard. When one gathering directs how the other is to dress, to think and to feel, when time isn't made for them or their companions. At the point when dread of that individual's temper demoralizes connections or closeness to other individuals. In a relationship where one gathering or different uses physical, verbal or enthusiastic mischief to drive collaboration and compliance isn't sound. None of these are solid signs in a relationship. Dread, melancholy and fury are not and ought not be a customary piece of any relationship. Indeed, individuals will blow up and dismal through the typical course of things, however when it is consistent, and it accomplishes a degree of 'misuse' - the relationship isn't sound.

Mental and Emotional Abuse: Misuse doesn't need to be physical, although when individuals consider misuse they think about the wounds and the wounds. Mental and psychological mistreatment is far crueler, leaves a lot of further injuries and isn't constantly obvious. For instance, Michael and Jane are dating. Michael sought after Jane overwhelmingly even while she was engaged with another man. He begged her on twisted knee to bring him into her life. Induced, Jane at long last did as such. From the outset, everything is extraordinary, and they share a great deal of exercises, yet he is consistently the person who chooses where they will go, what they will do and when they will do it. She wouldn't fret since she appreciates the consideration. On the off chance that she offers a proposal, he rushes to stigmatize the thought or to laugh at it. He will regularly reject her recommendations inside and out because he's now decided whether she thought about them or not. Jane realizes he does these things since he thinks about her, he discloses to her this constantly, yet Jane is reluctant to make any arrangements except if she gets notification from him first since he will get steamed.

This is a genuine model; it's a circumstance that deteriorated and more awful until a large portion of Jane's companions never observed Jane any longer. Her family occasionally observed her at all without Michael and just when Michael concluded that the time had come to visit with them. Her companions were shocked to find that for a long time, Michael 'separated' with Jane but, he never let her proceed onward on the grounds that he continued saying that he truly loved her and that in the long run, they would get back together. Michael used to make Jane feel horrendous if she needed to make her very own arrangements or did whatever did exclude him. He made her vibe dumb if she lounged around and hung tight for him to call all night notwithstanding when he had no aims of doing as such. Michael and Jane shared an extremely unfortunate relationship and it took many, numerous months for her to try and admit to anybody her annoyed considerably less offer what was occurring. In doing as such, Jane opened an entryway to an exit plan, however, went through an additional a while weakened by blame since she needed to be out. Michael didn't hit Jane. He never left a physical imprint on her. However, his states of mind, impulses and route with words held her powerless to resist him. At the point when gone up against by stressed companions with confirmation of Michael's disloyalties and different connections, Jane still couldn't cut off the association since Michael revealed to her it was all untruths - that the ladies made no difference to him and she was being deluded by her family and companions. As hard all things considered for certain individuals to accept, Jane trusted him.

Undesirable connections are a perilous thing since they don't need to be abrasive, messy and loaded up with physical punches to scar the individuals who become involved with them. Michael and Jane's model is just one, there are truly many others and for the individuals who have never had the setback to wind up in a terrible relationship it is extremely hard to fathom why anybody would remain in it. The reasons why these connections continue aren't just about the manipulative intensity of the other party, however the inborn want we have for enthusiastic closeness to other people. We need to be adored. We need to feel close. Notwithstanding when we fear what it is regardless, we need it to cherish us.

SIGNS A RELATIONSHIP WILL NOT LAST

Desire: In the special night stage, it's ordinary to get cleared up in an enthusiastic tornado of desire and feel like you can't get enough of your new accomplice. In any case, on the off chance that you have an inclination that your relationship depends entirely on this extraordinary, energetic, got to-make them feel, and there's not a great deal else you share practically speaking, that is an indication that things won't last when the hot vibes fail out.

On the off chance that the passionate high from the enthusiasm is the main thing holding you and your accomplice together, the relationship is in danger. On the off chance that you 'fell head over heels in adoration' you can simply drop out of affection. Clutching your accomplice as the enthusiastic love decreases, when there is no other paste in the relationship, doesn't work obviously, because the more tightly you hold, the more dangerous your accomplice moves toward becoming. On the off chance that you have regular interests and empathic correspondence, that is the paste that can hold a relationship together even after the enthusiasm winds down."

You Feel Like You Can't Fully Be Yourself: For a relationship to keep going long haul, it's so imperative to feel like you can generally be your real, bona fide self around your accomplice. On the off chance that you just began dating, it may take a bit for you to open up, and that is OK yet on the off chance that you wind up tread lightly in case you mistake and uncover some portion of yourself you would prefer not to impart to your accomplice, that is unsustainable over the long haul.

Your Partner Communicates Infrequently: Each couple has various benchmarks for how much or little they speak with one another, yet in the start of a relationship, it doesn't look good for the future in the event that you have a feeling that your accomplice doesn't organize you, and imparts less every now and again than you'd like.

"While nearly everybody can without much of a stretch say that they are occupied, when you find that somebody isn't being responsive from the get-go in the relationship, it may be an indication that they don't organize you, or connections all in all," Erika Bossiere, LMFT and Founder of The Relationship Institute of San Francisco, tells Bustle. "There are no hard guidelines on how 'responsive' somebody should be, and it's similarly critical to be tolerant. In any case, recollect, don't be excessively tolerant with somebody who will wind up squandering your time."

You Don't Like Their Friends: The organization we keep says a ton regarding our identity, and in the event that you understand right off the bat that you can't stand your accomplice's companions, that could show that you're not so much good long haul.

Not liking their friends is a tremendous marker that the relationship may be set out toward beset waters. Most importantly we picked our companions, and intermittently, we picked individuals that are like us here and there. On the off chance that you find that you don't care for their companions, know that your most up to date love may have a few characteristics in a portion of those kinships you don't care for.

You Notice Your Partner Adopting All Your Interests: In any long-haul relationship, the two accomplices should be free somewhat, and have their own remarkable advantages and pastimes that are isolated from their accomplice. On the off chance that you see that your new accomplice promptly attempts to embrace no different interests as you, that could be a warning that they'll be excessively reliant on you for their bliss later on.

"We discover accomplices that are like us, and furthermore, we search for the individuals who are not quite the same as us," Boissiere says. "Be watchful that when your lover suddenly changes into every one of your preferences, this may be a warning. You cherish drama? Suddenly, they do also. You adore hounds? What do you know, abruptly they have a young doggie? You like swing moving? They've joined up with five classes. At the point when the twin ship is excessively solid, the other accomplice frequently gets exhausted or suspicious of the other accomplice's intention. All things considered, we like individuals for their very own uniqueness, not our indistinguishable match."

Your Feel Like Your Opinion Isn't Valued: The establishment for any solid long-haul relationship is common regard, which implies that both accomplice's assessments are similarly esteemed in some random circumstance. On the off chance that you get the sense that your accomplice esteems their very own assessment over yours, that is a sign they won't make an extraordinary accomplice long haul.

You Accept Their Faults, But They Don't Accept Yours

The more you're with somebody, the better you'll become more acquainted with the 'genuine' them — which incorporates getting to know each other's issues and idiosyncrasies. On the off chance that your new accomplice has an issue with a portion of your not exactly consummate characteristics, however, anticipates that you should thoroughly acknowledge them without any inquiries posed, that doesn't look good for your sentimental future together.

If the other individual anticipates that you should pardon and tolerating of their shortcomings, yet they are not excusing or tolerating of yours, this isn't sensible. Nobody is immaculate, and we have deficiencies that should be acknowledged. If you will be there for them, they should be there for you also.

They Treat Others Poorly: In another relationship, everybody will be on their absolute best conduct, which implies that you should focus on how your accomplice treats you, yet everyone around the person in question — on the grounds that odds are that is the means by which they'll treat you one day, as well.

Right off the bat in a relationship, individuals treat their accomplices incredible, because the two gatherings are enamored," David Bennett, Certified Counselor, Relationship Expert, and Owner of The Popular Man and The Popular Teen, tells Bustle. "Be that as it may, take a gander at how your accomplice treats others their family, companions, and especially administration staff, similar to clerks and servers. In the long run, when the adoration blurs, they'll treat you along these lines, ensured."

They're Still Stuck On An Ex It ought to abandon saying, yet in the event that your new accomplice appears to at present be stuck on an regardless of whether everything they do is discussion gravely about the person in question that is a noteworthy warning that they aren't keen on or prepared for a long haul future with you. Stalking their ex via web-based networking media? Becoming involved with show with the ex? Perhaps wandering off in fantasy land about them? These are altogether terrible signs," Bennett says. "This implies their heart genuinely has a place with their ex. If so, all it will take is one occurrence where the ex is extra 'decent' or returns to cut off the association. Toward the day's end, it's up to you (and just you) to choose what your deal breakers in another relationship are. For whatever length of time that you're mindful of what you do and don't need in a long haul accomplice, and are keen enough to see any early warnings that your new accomplice probably won't be what you need over the long haul, there's no motivation behind why you won't have a cheerful, effective relationship regardless of whether you need to dump a couple of duds en route.

Effects of personality traits on a relationship

The thought that individuals contrast in their trademark methods for managing the world is one of the most fundamental human instincts. The antiquated Greeks accepted that the equalization of organic liquids (humors) decided an individual's fundamental character. Later hypotheses connected character to date of birth, skull shape, and body structure, yet these thoughts have neglected to discover observational help.

A progressively strong and deductively upheld hypothesis of character developed during the 1980s. As per The Big Five methodology, human character comprises of five fundamental qualities, every one of which exists on a continuum between contrary energies. The blend of these five characteristics in an individual predicts the individual's run of the mill conduct in various circumstances and after some time. The five noteworthy qualities are:

Neuroticism—nervousness and unpredictability versus enthusiastic strength and certainty;

Good faith—constancy and duty versus messiness and lethargy;

Appropriateness—kind disposition and compassion versus threatening vibe and impoliteness;

Receptiveness to encounter—inventiveness and interest versus bigotry and inflexibility;

Extroversion—decisiveness and criticalness versus introspection and timidity.

These qualities are hereditarily based. They will in general take shape in early adulthood and stay pretty much stable from that point. Character isn't the main factor forming our predetermination: Circumstances—situational, social, and verifiable—additionally have a great deal to do with it, as do possibility and life systems, obviously. However, the impact of character is apparent in numerous domains of life, for example, profession decision, wellbeing status, and way of life. As anyone might expect, the exploration writing likewise indicates a critical prescient relationship between the Big Five-character attributes and sentimental life.

Here is an unpleasant sketch of those discoveries.

Neuroticism

By a wide (and uncommon) academic agreement, neuroticism is the character characteristic most firmly prescient of an individual's sentimental fate. High neuroticism is consistently awful news in this unique circumstance. For instance, in 1987 University of Michigan specialists Lowell Kelly and James Connelly distributed an investigation that pursued 300 wedded couples more than 30 years. The neuroticism of one life partner anticipated disappointment in marriage and separation. Compounding an already painful situation, inquire about has additionally demonstrated that high neuroticism predicts low versatility post separate.

Neuroticism seems to meddle with relationship fulfillment in various ways. By definition, psychotic people will in general be profoundly receptive to stress and inclined to encountering pessimistic feelings. These inclinations are probably going to transmit onto the accomplice and make issues after some time.

Neuroticism likewise seems to meddle with sound sexuality. Terri Fisher at Ohio State University and James McNulty Florida State University (2008) got some information about their character, connections, and sexual fulfillment. After a year, the analysts came back to look at the nature of the connections of couples. They found that neuroticism of one accomplice (or both) anticipated lower levels of fulfillment seeing someone and sex. Neuroticism, the analysts further discovered, would in general undermine conjugal quality by meddling with the couple's sexual coexistence. The creators fight that neuroticism hoses sexual fulfillment since masochist people are inclined to contrary effect and desires, which have been appeared to identify with lower sexual excitement and fulfillment.

For the individuals who wish for a touch of existential flavor in their illustrative sauce, Jamie Goldenberg and partners contend that neuroticism may meddle with one's sexual coexistence to some extent on the grounds that "the creaturely parts of sex make obvious our creature nature, which helps us to remember our defenselessness and mortality." Neurotics are remarkably badly prepared to deal with this update and are hence headed to maintain a strategic distance from or cheapen sex.

Principles and Agreeableness

As may be normal, elevated amounts of uprightness and suitability anticipate relationship fulfillment, to some extent on the grounds that these qualities connote low impulsivity and high relational trust, separately.

Character therapist Portia Dyrenforth and partners (2010) distributed an investigation of 20,000 couples in three nations—Australia, England, and Germany—finding that high suitability and good faith (just as low neuroticism) in self or mate were related with conjugal fulfillment. Low suitability and low principles have been found to explicitly foresee sexual hazard taking. In an investigation of in excess of 16,000 members from 52 nations, the analyst David Schmidt of Bradley University found that low degrees of appropriateness and good faith anticipated disloyalty.

Receptiveness to Experience: Receptiveness seems to assume a fairly minor job in the sentimental setting. In 2010, the Australian scientist John Malouff and his associates dissected the consequences of 19 studies including in excess of 3,800 members. Four qualities; low neuroticism, high uprightness, high pleasantness, and high extraversion, anticipated larger amounts of relationship fulfillment with private accomplices. Discoveries identifying with transparency were MIA.

However, transparency isn't totally immaterial: Researchers Andrea Meltzer and James McNulty of Florida State University as of late solicited 278 sets from love birds to keep an everyday log of their sexual exercises for about fourteen days. Respondents were additionally examined concerning their characters and the nature of their relationship. One of their discoveries was that the lady's character anticipated the recurrence of sexual relations in the marriage. In particular, couples in which the lady scored high on the characteristics of pleasantness and (to a lesser degree) transparency engaged in sexual relations all the more regularly. The spouse's character had no impact on the recurrence of sex, albeit progressively open (and psychotic) husbands were less explicitly fulfilled.

Since numerous investigations have just demonstrated that men when in doubt look for more incessant and differed sex than ladies, the scientists' conjecture that the lady is generally the "guardian" for sex in the marriage and decides whether and how regularly it will occur.

Extroversion

Extroversion has been found to unequivocally foresee a few love and sex-related results. In any case, high extroversion has all the earmarks of being to some degree a twofold edged sword in this specific situation. Outgoing individuals will in general be more joyful, all the more socially associated, and more appealing than contemplative people. They look for relations and are talented at dealing with them. They additionally will in general be better balanced explicitly.

Then again, high extroversion can undermine connections since it is related with adventurism. A recent report by David Schmidt including in excess of 13,000 members in 46 nations observed high extroversion to be "emphatically corresponded with enthusiasm for transient mating, unhindered sapiosexuality, having occupied with momentary mate poaching endeavors, having surrendered to transient poaching endeavors of others, and lacking relationship selectiveness."

In an investigation of since quite a while ago wedded couples, Arlene Rosowski of Harvard and associates found that high extroversion and low reliability in men anticipated lower conjugal fulfillment for their spouses. In opposition to mainstream thinking, couples don't turn out to be increasingly comparative in character as they age together; rather, individuals will in general select accomplices who are very such as themselves. Truth be told, explore has demonstrated that individuals will in general pick accomplices who take after them over numerous areas, a marvel known as assortative mating. As a rule, with regards to match holding, similar people are attracted to each other.

Strikingly, this propensity can effectively affect society. Affluent individuals will in general wed other well-off individuals. Profoundly taught individuals will in general wed other very instructed individuals. In a general public like our own, where instruction and lucrative employments are accessible for both genders, social holes in pay, status, and accomplishment will undoubtedly develop quick, as the rich and profoundly taught progressively mate with one another.

With regards to character, our insight into the human inclination to look for likeness in a mate brings up the issue: Does character similitude between mates anticipate more joyful marriage? The appropriate response: Probably not.

Without a doubt, some proof exists that similitude predicts relationship fulfillment. Shanhong Luo (2009) pursued 117 recently dating couples and found that a likeness in character attributes anticipated higher relationship fulfillment.

Nonetheless, the majority of the proof seems to demonstrate that likeness is definitely not a solid indicator of relationship result. Portia Dyrenforth and partners found no connection between the level of comparability of the couple's characters and fulfillment in marriage. In an ongoing investigation of in excess of 1600 couples, Swiss analyst Katrin Furler and her associates found no connection between character likeness and life fulfillment.

It is conceivable that the significance of character similitude changes over the life of the relationship. Michelle Shiota of the University of Arizona and Robert Levenson at the University of California, Berkeley (2007) found that while comparative character predicts higher relationship fulfillment among youthful wedded couples, among more seasoned couples, comparability in the huge five noteworthy characteristics anticipated decreased fulfillment.

Our fundamental character attributes are under solid hereditary impact and are difficult to change. Character predicts conduct in numerous regions, including relationship, sexual conduct, and fulfillment. High neuroticism is plainly hazardous in this unique circumstance. Conversely, appropriateness and reliability are unambiguously positive characteristics. Receptiveness seems to assume a minor job, and extroversion has a blended pack quality, with both positive and negative ramifications for connections. In opposition to mainstream thinking, character closeness between mates isn't important for long haul relationship achievement.

In general, the information recommends that the individuals who are searching for an accomplice for suffering affection and sex need not focus on discovering somebody like them in character. Or maybe, they'd profit by searching for an accomplice who's pleasing, principled, and genuinely steady. An outgoing accomplice may demonstrate a bundle bargain: It'll be fun; however, it probably won't end well. An excessively masochist accomplice is a solicitation to the blues.

Perceiving a portion of these character attributes in yourself or your accomplice may make you dread for the long-haul wellbeing and sexual joy of your relationship. Yet, it's helpful to recollect that an individual may choose to change, improve their propensities, and better deal with their designed character inclinations through mindfulness, practice, and a craving to have their direct express the qualities they regard commendable.

Chapter Five

COMMUNICATION IN A RELATIONSHIP

Communication

Communication is the exchange of data starting with one spot then onto the next. Seeing someone, correspondence permits to you disclose to another person what you are encountering and what your needs are. The demonstration of imparting addresses your issues; however, it additionally encourages you to be associated in your relationship.

Imparting clearly in a relationship

Converse with one another. Regardless of how well you know and cherish one another, you can't peruse your accomplice's brain. We have to convey plainly to maintain a strategic distance from false impressions that may cause hurt, outrage, hatred or disarray. It takes two individuals to have a relationship and every individual has distinctive correspondence needs and styles. Couples need to discover a method for imparting that suits their relationship. Solid correspondence styles require practice and diligent work, anyway correspondence will never be flawless constantly. Be clear when speaking with your accomplice, so your message can be gotten and comprehended. Twofold check your comprehension of what your accomplice is stating.

When you converse with your accomplice, attempt to:

Put aside time to talk without interference from other individuals or diversions like telephones, PCs or TV consider what you need to state, be clear about what you need to convey, make your message obvious, with the goal that your accomplice hears it precisely and comprehends what you mean, talk about what's going on and how it influences you talk about what you need, need and feel – use 'I' articulations, for example, 'I need', 'I need' and 'I feel' acknowledge duty regarding your own emotions tune in to your accomplice. Set aside your own musings until further notice and attempt to comprehend their expectations, sentiments, needs and needs (this is called sympathy) share positive emotions with your accomplice, for example, what you acknowledge and appreciate about them, and that they are so essential to you know about your manner of speaking arrange and recall that you don't need to be correct constantly. If the issue you are having isn't that significant, here and there let the issue go, or settle on a truce.

Non-verbal correspondence: When we convey, we can say a great deal without talking. Our body pose, manner of speaking and the appearances all over all pass on a message. These non-verbal methods for conveying can tell the other individual how we feel about them. If our sentiments don't fit with our words, it is frequently the non-verbal correspondence that gets 'heard' and accepted. For instance, saying 'I adore you' to your accomplice in a level, exhausted, manner of speaking, gives two altogether different messages. Notice whether your non-verbal communication reflects what you are stating.

Tuning in and correspondence: Listening is a significant piece of successful correspondence. A decent audience can urge their accomplice to talk transparently and genuinely. Tips for good listening include: keep agreeable eye to eye connection, lean towards the other individual and make signals to show intrigue and concern have an open, non-protective, genuinely loosened up stance with your arms and legs uncrossed face the other individual – don't sit or stand sideways sit or remain on a similar level to abstain from gazing upward to or down on the other individual abstain from diverting signals, for example, squirming with a pen, looking at papers, or tapping your feet or fingers know that physical obstructions, commotion or intrusions will make great correspondence troublesome. Quiet phones or other specialized gadgets to guarantee you are truly tuning in give the other individual a chance to talk without interference show authentic consideration and intrigue utilize self-assured articulations like 'I feel …. about … ', 'What I need is… ' know about your tone be set up to invest significant energy in the event that you are feeling extremely furious about something. It may be smarter to quiet down before you address the issue request criticism from the other individual on your tuning in.

Improving correspondence in a relationship: Open and clear correspondence can be educated. A few people think that it's difficult to talk and may need time and support to express their perspectives. These individuals might be great audience members, or they might be individuals whose activities talk more intense than their words.

You can improve your correspondence by:

Building brotherhood, sharing encounters, interests and worries with your accomplice, and indicating fondness and appreciation, sharing closeness – closeness isn't just a sexual association. Closeness is made by having snapshots of inclination close and joined to your accomplice. It means having the option to comfort and be ameliorated, and to be transparent. A demonstration of closeness can be as straightforward as bringing your accomplice some tea since you can tell they are worn out; being on a similar page as your accomplice. It's significant that you and your accomplice are both in concession to key issues in your relationship, for example, how funds are conveyed, what key objectives you have, and your child rearing styles.

To improve the way you impart, begin by posing inquiries, for example; What things cause strife among you and your accomplice? It is safe to say that they are on the grounds that you are not tuning in to one another.

What things bring you joy and sentiments of association?

What things cause you frustration and agony?

What things don't you talk about and what stops you discussing them?

How might you like your correspondence with your accomplice to appear as something else?

On the off chance that conceivable, pose these inquiries with your accomplice and offer your reactions. Consider, and attempt, approaches to convey in an unexpected way. See whether the outcomes improve your correspondence. When you are increasingly mindful of how you convey, you will most likely have more authority over what occurs between you. While it may not be simple from the start, opening new regions of correspondence can prompt an all the more satisfying relationship.

A large portion of us discover a few encounters or points hard to discuss. It might be something that is difficult or makes us feel awkward. For instance, a few people think that it's hard to express their feelings. It is frequently the things that can't be discussed that hurt the most. If you are experiencing issues conveying everything that needs to be conveyed, or chatting with your accomplice about something, you may discover it converses with an instructor.

Overseeing strife with correspondence

Abstain from utilizing the quiet treatment.

Try not to form a hasty opinion. Discover every one of the realities instead of speculating thought processes.

Talk about what really occurred. Try not to pass judgment.

Figure out how to see one another, not to crush one another.

Talk utilizing the future and current state, not the past tense.

Focus on the serious issue, and don't get diverted by other minor issues.

Discussion about the issues that hurt your or your accomplice's emotions, at that point proceed onward to issues about contrasts in sentiments.

Use 'I feel' explanations, not 'You are' proclamations.

Looking for assistance for correspondence issues. On the off chance that you can't improve the correspondence in your relationship, think about conversing with a relationship instructor. Guides are prepared to perceive the examples in a couple's correspondence that is causing issues and to help change those examples. You could likewise consider completing a course that is important to your relationship. It is smarter to act early and converse with somebody about your worries, as opposed to hold up until things deteriorate.

How to Improve Communication in Romantic Relationships

Undesirable verbal correspondence regularly begins with negative contemplations or troublesome feelings as opposed to words. On the off chance that you are in a long-haul sentimental relationship, you have invested enough energy with your accomplice to feel like you know them back to front. You envision how they respond in specific circumstances, notwithstanding, your concept of their identity may prompt passing up on a chance to re-find them. This frequently negatively affects how we impart in a sentimental relationship connection are tied in with staying inquisitive about who the other individual truly is and how they see the world. Be that as it may, after such a significant number of years, how might you see your accomplice from an alternate perspective? Marva

Collins, an American teacher known for her extreme however deferential showing strategies, has worked with devastated and grieved understudies who have a difficult time prevailing in school. Her encouraging strategies helped them to succeed. Her methodology is significant in any relationship.

Toward the start of every semester, Collins would try to tell students that they had effectively gotten their evaluations for the school year ahead. She disclosed to them that they had all gotten good grades and their activity during the semester was to ensure they did everything not to lose this standing. So instead of having the understudies demonstrate to her that they had the option to get top evaluations, she demonstrated to them that she put stock in them—that they were deserving of the best training. This demonstrated to be profoundly rousing and moving (Collins and Tamarkin, 1990). Collins' methodology depended on making the correct discernment for herself as well as other people. She would regard understudies as though they were top Harvard graduates, as long as they didn't demonstrate her generally. Understudies started with her full trust, consolation, and appreciation. Accept simply the best for your accomplice. Put them on a platform for being so extraordinary and after that discussion to them in a proper manner. Wouldn't you like to be addressed as though you were esteemed, acknowledged, regarded, and adored regardless? Accordingly, how might you respond to somebody who had a favorable opinion of you? What comes around goes around. You will see your correspondence improve radically.

How to solve communication issues

Struggle in a relationship is practically unavoidable. In itself, struggle isn't an issue; how it's taken care of, be that as it may, can unite individuals or destroy them. Poor relational abilities, differences, and errors can be a wellspring of displeasure and separation or a springboard to a more grounded relationship and more joyful future. Next time you're managing struggle, remember these tips on compelling relational abilities and you can make a progressively positive result. Here's the secret.

Remain Focused: In some cases, it's enticing to raise past apparently related clashes when managing current ones. It feels pertinent to address everything that is irritating you without a moment's delay and get everything discussed while you're as of now managing one clash. Tragically, this frequently mists the issue and makes discovering shared comprehension and an answer for the present issue more outlandish and makes the entire exchange all the more exhausting and notwithstanding confounding. Try not to raise past damages or different subjects. Remain concentrated on the present, your emotions, understanding each other and finding an answer. Rehearsing care reflection can assist you with learning to be progressively present in all aspects of your life.

Listen Carefully: Individuals regularly believe they're tuning in yet are truly pondering what they're going to state next when the other individual quits talking. Truly compelling correspondence goes the two different ways. While it may be troublesome, attempt truly tuning in to what your accomplice is stating. Try not to intrude. Try not to get cautious. Simply hear them and reflect back what they're stating so they realize you've heard. At that point you'll comprehend them better and they'll be additionally eager to hear you out. These procedures can assist you with becoming an increasingly successful audience.

Attempt to See Their Point of View: In a contention, most of us essentially need to feel heard and comprehended. We gab about our perspective to get the other individual to see things our way. This is justifiable, however a lot of an emphasis all alone want to be comprehended to the exclusion of everything else can reverse discharge. Unexpectedly, if we do this constantly, there's little spotlight on the other individual's perspective, and no one feels comprehended. Attempt to truly observe the opposite side, and afterward you can more likely clarify yours. (On the off chance that you don't 'get it', pose more inquiries until you do.) Others will more probable tune if they feel heard. These psychological bends once in a while make it hard to see different perspectives. Are any of them well-known?

React to Criticism with Empathy: When somebody comes at you with analysis, it's anything but difficult to feel that they're off-base and get cautious. While analysis is difficult to hear and regularly overstated or shaded by the other individual's feelings, it's critical to tune in to the next individual's agony and react with sympathy for their emotions. Likewise, search for what's valid in what they're stating; that can be important data for you. Peruse progressively about developing sympathy and absolution.

Possess What's Yours: Understand that moral obligation is a quality, not a shortcoming. Successful correspondence includes conceding when you're off-base. On the off chance that you both offer some obligation in a contention (which is typically the situation), search for and admit to what's yours. It diffuses the circumstance, sets a genuine model, and shows development. It likewise regularly rouses the other individual to react in kind, driving you both closer to shared comprehension and an answer.

Use "I" Messages: As opposed to making statements like, "You truly wrecked here," start proclamations with "I", and make them about yourself and your sentiments, like, "I feel baffled when this occurs." It's less accusatory, starts less protectiveness, and enables the other individual to comprehend your perspective as opposed to feeling assaulted. Study, "I message" and other confident correspondence methods.

Search for Compromise: Rather than attempting to win the contention, search for arrangements that address everyone's issues. Either through trade off or another innovative arrangement that gives you both what you need most, this center is considerably more powerful than one individual getting what they need at the other's cost. Solid correspondence includes finding a goal that the two sides can be content with.

Take a Time-Out: Occasionally tempers get warmed and it's simply too hard to even consider continuing a talk without it turning into a contention or a battle. In the event that you feel yourself or your accomplice beginning to persuade too irate to be in any way valuable, or demonstrating some dangerous correspondence designs, it's alright to take a break from the talk until you both chill. This can mean going for a stroll and chilling to come back to the discussion in 30 minutes, "thinking about it" so you can process what you're feeling somewhat more, or whatever feels like the best fit for you two, as long as you do come back to the discussion. Now and then great correspondence means realizing when to take a break.

Try not to Give Up: While taking a break from the exchange is now and then a smart thought, consistently return to it. On the off chance that you both methodology the circumstance with a helpful mentality, shared regard, and a readiness to see the other's perspective or if nothing else discover an answer, you can gain ground toward the objective of a goals to the contention. Except if it's an ideal opportunity to abandon the relationship, don't abandon correspondence.

Request Help If You Need It: On the off chance that either of you experiences difficulty remaining deferential during struggle or in the event that you've given settling strife with your accomplice a shot your very own and the circumstance simply doesn't appear to improve, you may profit by a couple of sessions with an advisor. Couples directing or family treatment can furnish help with fights and instruct abilities to determine future clash. On the off chance that your accomplice wouldn't like to go, you can in any case regularly advantage from going alone.

Important questions to ask before getting into a relationship

A significant number of my patients have approached me when it is suitable for them to discover vital data about somebody they are considering proceeding to date. They need to know right off the bat if they ought to contribute the time and vitality that a quality relationship requires. The point at which you are not yet put resources into the result. That implies as from the get-go in another relationship as you can. Their next evident concern is the sorts of inquiries they should need replied.

There are numerous things you could ask that would pick up you the data you need, however there are ten intense and effective information social affair addresses that effectively start the procedure of truly knowing someone's identity. Since they are profoundly close request, it is additionally significant that you approach your potential accomplice from genuine interest and an adoration for common investigation.

If you both are keen on realizing what you can anticipate from one another in a personal, long haul relationship, you ought to be promptly eager to be similarly as open consequently. Being eager to be as legit as you are capable will give you the most obvious opportunity with regards to making a heads-up about what your odds of progress are down the line.

Following are ten inquiries that are frequently fruitful initiators of a solid start, alongside certain clarifications and models. As you experience them, investigate what your own responses and answers would be were you to be on the opposite finish of somebody who is searching for a similar sort of real closeness.

How are you when you don't get what you need?

We are probably going to have explicit wants of our partners that are probably not going to be met after some time. Those failure frequently bring about dissatisfaction and pity. Individuals who are adaptable, sure, and imaginative don't respond with indignation, pushiness, or endeavors to control. Rather, they will discuss why their solicitation is critical to them or offer to consult by giving something consequently. In the case of nothing works, they rely upon their own assets and don't rebuff.

Extraordinary answer: "I'm humiliated to state that I some of the time frown a bit, however I could never need my accomplice to accomplish something she would not like to. There are a lot of different approaches to get what you need."

Luke-warm answer: "It depends whether it's extremely imperative to me and my accomplice could give it on the off chance that he needed to, however is retaining in light of the fact that he's distraught about something different. I can surrender it if it will be a genuine issue, however not until the end of time."

Cautioning sign: "If it's significant, I push until I get my direction. It's quite reasonable."

In the event that you can't help contradicting your accomplice about something significant, what strategies do you normally use to persuade the person in question to be your ally?

Contradictions occur in all connections. Individuals originate from different foundations with numerous layers of both agonizing and prized recollections that are showed in each new association. As individuals become more acquainted with one another, they experience predispositions and biased demeanors of their accomplice's frames of mind and practices. Contingent upon how profoundly settled in those inclinations are, either accomplice may utilize various practices to get the other individual to see it his or her way.

Extraordinary answer: "The best arrangement is for the two of us to listen cautiously to what different feels and thinks and after that attempts to discover shared conviction. Now and then I need to give way, and some of the time he does."

Luke-warm answer: "I give her each possibility I can to persuade me that she's correct, however on the off chance that she can't, I anticipate that her should come over on to my side."

Cautioning sign: "On the off chance that he needs to differ with me over something that is extremely significant, I normally simply step back and imagine I couldn't care less. I settle the score with him in different ways when he's into power and control."

If your accomplice approaches you for something you can't or don't have any desire to give, do you accuse the person in question for needing it from you?

Individuals who tend towards supposing they ought to naturally give whatever their accomplices needs can feel that they are not measuring up on the off chance that they can't, or may not need, to give it. To feel less remorseful, they frequently are disturbed they are placed in that situation at all and censure their accomplices for needing it in any case. That is particularly valid for new darlings who need to be everything to one another. Now and again what one individual need is basically not accessible from the other, in spite of profound sentiments of affection. Fault ought to never be the reaction.

Extraordinary answer: "That would be simple yet in no way, shape or form reasonable. On the off chance that I need something, and she isn't into it, it's never her deficiency. I would make it truly clear that it is so essential to me yet fault never illuminates anything."

Luke-warm answer: "I make an effort not to consider me to be as the trouble maker on the off chance that he can't give me something I need, in any case, genuinely, most folks who are truly in to you make a decent attempt, whatever you ask, wouldn't you say?"

Cautioning sign: "In the event that she doesn't attempt, is there any good reason why I wouldn't accuse her? She needs to keep her needs straight in the event that she needs me to continue cherishing her the manner in which she needs consequently."

Would you say you are available to better approaches for seeing things regardless of whether they struggle with your own feelings?

New sweethearts normally center around the manners in which they feel the equivalent about everything. They need one heartbeat, one dream, and one way. They will in general disregard or stifle any real contrasts that could compromise that shared reality. However, in the long run they will surface. At the point when stood up to with another thought that may challenge a built-up view, most accomplices will do whatever they can to determine their disparities as fast as would be prudent. Sadly, that may not generally be a relationship-positive reaction. Couples with the most obvious opportunity to work through those unique thoughts listen in all respects cautiously to one another before they react.

Incredible answer: "I had a father that was a self-declared definer of the real world. It didn't make a difference what you thought or felt, it was forever his way or the thruway. I'm a genuine adherent that my accomplice will consistently have a great deal to show me and the other way around. You can generally return to what you think, yet it's incredible to take a gander at things from an alternate perspective."

Luke-warm answer: "Well, I need to concede, I have some solid suppositions on things that are essential to me. I'd generally tune in, yet I'm difficult to persuade."

Cautioning sign: "I put a great deal of time and vitality into what I think and do. I don't care for it when somebody attempts to disclose to me that I don't have a clue what I'm discussing. Individuals need to stay with what they know and what works for them. It takes a hellfire of a contention to cause me to tune in to something that doesn't feel right."

When something is essential to you, what procedures do you frequently use to get your accomplice to do what you need?

At the point when individuals have powerful urges for something they need and are worried that their accomplices may not be happy to offer it to them, their reactions can run the range from frowning, retaining, pushiness, beguile, bothering, detachment, affliction, arrangement, or asking. The accomplices on the opposite end may have identical reactions gained from their own past relationship, psychological weight that can incredibly impact the result.

Incredible answer: "Well, cajoling first, obviously. You can get progressively out of anybody you adore when you're caring in your methodology and not pushy. On the off chance that it's significant, I simply reveal to her why it is important so much and tune in to what she needs to like give me what I need. I'm a major mediator, not a pusher. Much better over the long haul."

Luke-warm answer: "It relies upon whether he has some credit at the time. In the event that he's been pleasant to me for some time, I'm bound to simply approach and seek after the best. In the event that he owes me one, I will get in there and battle on the off chance that I need to."

Cautioning sign: "I'm basically eager to do anything I need to if it's extremely imperative to me. I begin with a sensible style, yet I can get truly extraordinary in the event that I feel I'm being denied what I merit."

When you feel disengaged from your accomplice, what do you as a rule do to get back together?

Disengagements between darlings are very normal and, if not settled, can bring about a developing hole between them. At the point when defied with an excessive amount of disappointment or danger, a few people retreat to their corners to lick their enthusiastic injuries, sitting tight for the other to approach and apologize, or, at any rate, a harmony offering or some likeness thereof. Others forget about and figure things all alone, ideally to return when they feel prepared to interface once more. At times, the two accomplices solidify in their honesty and possibly return when they can never again bear being separated. Without goals, there have been no exercises learned and the example is too prone to even consider happening once more. Time after time, it is just one of the accomplices who attempts to get things in the groove again, and that lopsidedness will hurt the relationship over the long haul.

Extraordinary answer: "Whatever it takes. I despise being independent from her for exceptionally long. When we battle, it's ordinarily over something unimportant or something we've quite recently not invested the effort to fathom. I don't accept on retention love since I'm furious."

Luke-warm answer: "I have to ensure that he will be responsive. I don't care for being rejected and I'm not liable to get used to him except if he makes the principal move on the off chance that he wasn't right."

Cautioning sign: "I sit tight for her to make the move. I detest seeing it when folk's weakling out. At the point when a lady comes to you, she's a lot simpler to deal with during the make-up. You're bound to get what you need out of the arrangement."

Would you say you are straightforward with your accomplice about what you need in a relationship?

Over and over again in my I hear, "I can't disclose to him that. He'd never open up to me again." Or, "She's excessively touchy to what I need to state. She'll simply blow up, and after that cry. I generally wind up saying what she needs to hear."

New sweethearts for the most part intuit what different needs. They request what they feel will be seen by the different as proper or has the most obvious opportunity with regards to being allowed. That is the thing that gives them the undetectable radiance of an ideal match. After some time, different wants will undoubtedly develop whether undercover or obvious. In the event that individuals can't be straightforward in advance with what they need from a cozy accomplice, they will exhibit just what they feel will be acknowledged. That establishment of inauthenticity is a delicate one.

Trustworthiness isn't a reason for ugliness or assault. It is simply a way to pass on an individual's actual nature and what satisfies them. Without that data, no accomplice can realize how to give what is required.

Incredible answer: "Basically about anything. I'm somewhat restless in the event that I believe it will hurt her for reasons unknown and I do like my private considerations when I'm attempting to make sense of myself. In any case, anything she needs to decide on that is going to influence her, or us, totally."

Luke-warm answer: "More often than not. I think folks truly would prefer not to comprehend what ladies do to organize the result some of the time. They simply need the prize toward the end. In addition, I like folks to mind enough to make sense of me."

Cautioning sign: "Heck, no. All things considered, not what goes on in my psyche. I reveal to her what she has to know to fulfill what I need, yet the remainder of me is untouchable. I'm a person. Ladies don't get us in case we're excessively open."

Would you say you are dependable?

The vast majority promptly consider disloyalty; however, unfaithfulness is just a subset of breaking an understanding that two individuals have, at one time, made decisively. Those agreements are constantly open to arrangement, yet never to deliberate welching on the arrangement. In extraordinary connections, the two accomplices respect a special stepped area spot of their own creation, an option that is more noteworthy than themselves that both enthusiastically hold fast to. That special raised area spot is the confidence of their relationship, a position of conduct and however that both hold holy. On the off chance that either accomplice "breaks that confidence," they are being unfaithful to that which they have concurred.

Uninvolved forceful conduct, guarantee breaking, rehashed pardons over bombed compliancy, and mystery practices where the other accomplice doesn't get the chance to cast a ballot, are largely serious ruptures of trust. Obviously, there are extraordinary conditions, yet they are neither predictable nor incessant, and they lead to making another establishment where trust is more grounded.

Trust is the critical establishment of any great fellowship, business association, or cozy relationship.

Extraordinary answer: "I've committed a few errors throughout my life by supposing I could get around things, yet they generally exploded backward. I've truly discovered that keeping guarantees and being valid about your identity with the individual most essential to you are unpreventable certainties in any great relationship. My accomplice merits the best of me straight.

Luke-warm answer: "I've never comprehended what that truly implies. I'm only one out of every odd going to reveal to him stuff that may make him question his adoration for me except if there's no chance to get out of it. This should be relatively unimportant to him insofar as I'm sure about the significant stuff."

Cautioning sign: "She doesn't have to know it all about me. I like my autonomy and my opportunity. I'm extraordinary to her and what I do without anyone else is my business. I don't lie inside and out, yet I make it entirely evident that she takes what she sees, or I'm out of the relationship."

Do you clutch feelings of hatred?

It is critical that the accomplices in a personal relationship don't get behind on their enthusiastic Mastercard's. On the off chance that they store up feelings of hatred without goals, they will in the end have all the proof they have to retain love and sit tight for the other to "pay back" before they consider opening back up once more.

Feelings of disdain heap up and feed upon themselves. They can exponentially develop until there may not be a way home once more. A great many people who keep a reserve of old damages and frustrations have discovered that personal conduct standard in adolescence. It very well may be changed, yet just with duty and diligent work.

Incredible answer: "I attempt to relinquish negative stuff between us when I can. I've discovered that folks abhor repeating or annoying. I do need goals between us so a similar stuff doesn't come up again and again, yet keeping an overabundance of annoyance just prompts being hopeless inside and to him."

Luke-warm answer: "Some of the time. When she explodes and assaults at that point anticipates that me should simply be there at whatever point she's over it. I would prefer not to be pushed around, and simply give in effectively when it's helpful for her. When it takes her some time to get me back, she's smarter to me."

Cautioning sign: "When folks are mean, you need to tell them that you're cost goes up when they don't do what they should. I remain distraught until he unmistakably understands that he owes me one. I like the power."

How would you most regularly express your adoration for somebody?

It is right around a given that men frequently express their affection explicitly and by social caretaking, and ladies by enthusiastic following and expectation of their darling's needs. On the off chance that each concurs that those articulations are gotten and acknowledged, there isn't an issue. However, when either is progressively sexual, more needing enthusiastic sustenance, increasingly tender, or keener on hanging out than the other, at that point those distinctions are probably going to bring about dissatisfactions and disappointments.

Frequently it is simply a question of training each other what somebody implies by specific practices or approaching all the more explicitly for what works. Different occasions, each accomplice must interpret what the different says or does to acknowledge love communicated contrastingly that may feel additionally satisfying.

It is imperative to recollect and acknowledge that demonstrating love in a manner the other doesn't feel or need it might not have the positive outcomes that are wanted. Regularly accomplices will show love in a manner they might want it and not require some investment to interpret their words and practices into those their accomplices will involvement as adoring. Open correspondence is never more significant than in the manners in which love is communicated and experienced.

Incredible answer: "In the manner in which they can feel it. I realize that adoring somebody takes a ton of persistence to become more acquainted with what is important to them, not simply to me. I'm truly imaginative. I do tell my accomplice that I need her to be open and genuine in revealing to me what fulfills her."

Luke-warm answer: "I'm an extremely loving lady. I contact and touch constantly. It's imperative to me that my accomplice acknowledges how pleasant I am and lets me know so. I need that sort of minding back and I'm not a glad camper on the off chance that he doesn't do that."

Cautioning sign: "I like sex, period. I can do the various things ladies state they need, yet in the event that there's no gold toward the end, there's no rainbow. Snuggling is for children and creatures. People need to get it on."

As these ten inquiries are exhibited and replied by both potential accomplices, they can open the conduits for the numerous others that will ideally pursue. What's more, however it might appear to be hard and somewhat cumbersome to hazard asking them in advance, you will be amazed at how fruitful the outcomes will be.

HEALTHY RELATIONSHIP COMMUNICATION

Never under any circumstance talk about significant things on content

Or then again email, or phone message. Messaging has turned into a prop in our general public, and ought to be utilized for little, pointless things. Here's an indication: on the off chance that you are having a discussion of more than 5 or 6 messages forward and backward, it's a great opportunity to put down the telephone (or lift it up, on the off chance that you need to call). Messaging isn't generally a discussion; it's a progression of messages–as a rule not progressively that can be effectively misconstrued. We as a whole skill that renowned four-letter word, "Fine" can be confounded! Face to face, you can peruse facial signals, tone and non-verbal communication. What's more, it's much simpler to be cruel and unforgiving when you are conversing with a small-scale PC screen.

Be straightforward with one another

One of the most exceedingly terrible turns I've seen a relationship take is the point at which one (or both) individuals imagine they are glad for satisfying their accomplice or quieting them down. Suppose you feel awkward with your beau's new appealing work companion whom you've never met, however who has been going along with him for party time on a week after week premise. Converse with him about it. In spite of your apprehensions of being called desirous, controlling, insane or excessively touchy, it's smarter to be straightforward with your emotions. When you restrain things, it can prompt repressed dissatisfaction and blasts later on that can for all time harm connections.

Try not to raise issues when you will be inclined to tears or silly annoyance

Alright, so suppose you have an issue with your SO. Perhaps she's been disclosing to you that you aren't permitted to watch the game on Sundays, or possibly he isn't endeavoring to coexist with your people. You're most likely disturbed, irate, baffled… there's a lot of feelings going on. Be that as it may, despite the fact that feeling is the wellspring of contention, struggle doesn't need to be driven totally be it. Try not to raise your issue when you realize that you may turn to hollering or crying. It's harder to be discerning and see the two sides when tears are spilling down your face and four-letter words are flying out your mouth

All's reasonable in affection and couple battles

Skill to battle, it's as straightforward as that. It's begins with listening–genuinely tuning in to each other. Periodically, couples attempt and talk over one another so it turns into this sort of rivalry to the contention closure end goal (which may wind up with somebody on the love seat). Truly hear one out another, don't get awful or submit low blows. Low blows incorporate verbally abusing, affronts, raising the past or raising something that you realize will be a passionate trigger or "burrow."

Attempt and use "we" articulations, or "I feel proclamations" rather than accusatory "I" and ""your" explanations

You never ask me how my day was!" "You generally grumble about me!" "You never plan dates!" These announcements, however, they might be valid, look like assaults to the individual on the less than desirable end. Rather than pointing fingers, or deploring your own issues, attempt and recollect that a relationship is two individuals going about as one unit, not two totally separate people attempting to get their own specific manner.

Resolve strife with a hint of adoration

Most importantly, as I stated, clash is best settled face to face. Hold his hand, look at her without flinching, maybe even put an arm around one another. Physical contact will remind you both that the essential reason you are battling isn't for struggle of getting your direction, but since you both love and care about one another and need to have a more beneficial relationship.

Pick your fights

Nobody enjoys a grumbler or a whiner. So, suppose your lover completes a few vexatious things: he calls you late some of the time, he doesn't compliment you any longer and he depends on put-down during contentions. The last one ought to be tended to immovably and right away. The center one can be settled through some encouraging feedback. In any case, him forgetting about time since he was playing the new GTA? Release it. Life it excessively short, and an excessive amount of contention can get you named a bother

Struggle doesn't mean separation

Rehash after me: since you're contending now in your relationship, does not mean you should separate. Such huge numbers of couples end it since they've had seven days of roughness. As I would see it, in the event that you both cherish one another and there are no issues of duping, misuse, psychological well-being or outrageous incongruence issues, 9 out of multiple times it shouldn't need to prompt a separation. Keep in mind that each relationship has good and bad times. What's more, on the off chance that you're not willing to endure the hardship to see the daylight, at that point you will have bombed relationship after bombed relationship. The excellence of affection isn't in the dozen roses on Valentine's Day, or holding each other in the great occasions, it's in remaining together in spite of the blemishes.

Chapter Six

FINDING A SOULMATE

The idea of perfect partners is a polarizing one. All things considered, in a universe of 7 billion individuals, it's difficult to envision we each have just one impeccable match.

Be that as it may, numerous individuals who put stock in perfect partners don't characterize them along these lines. Or maybe, they accept a perfect partner is an individual whom you interface with right away and profoundly, who sees and acknowledges you for your identity and simultaneously, pushes you to develop into the best form of yourself.

A perfect partner doesn't need to be a sentimental association, fundamentally it could be a companion, relative or educator. Nor does the relationship should be simple constantly or free of contention.

"A perfect partner isn't constantly enclosed by the ideal bundle, physically or as far as life conditions — nor does it imply that the relationship will come without difficulties," Kailen Rosenberg, author of The Lodge Social Club, told HuffPost. "However, the thing that matters is that the existence conditions and the troublesome difficulties are a reinforcing power that turns into the paste that keeps you together through the troublesome occasions and enables every one of you to turn into your most bona fide self."

What will show you that you have met your ideal partner?

Being around this individual gives you a feeling of harmony and solace, even in all respects from the get-go in the relationship.

Whenever I initially met my partner after at first interfacing on, when our eyes met, I wasn't on edge or anxious about gathering some outsider off the web. It resembled that tune verse, 'It is well with my spirit,' something about him quickly felt natural and I was in a flash settled simply being in his essence. I didn't get the butterflies around this extraordinarily ravishing person who couldn't take his eyes off me; rather, it resembled my spirit remembered him as my missing piece. When we met the first occasion when, it truly resembled time stopped and all I could hear was my heart beating, everything I could see was him.

You might be altogether different, yet you balance each other out.

I realized my significant other was my perfect partner when I understood the manners in which we were inverse adjusted me and the manners in which we were indistinguishable bettered me. It's an adrenaline-powered, strange inclination that is additionally dazzling in a how are you so ideal for me kind of way.

You get this obvious hunch that you've met your match.

When I met my perfect partner, I had no clue what a perfect partner truly was — other than what the joyfully ever-after society instructs us. I was on an excursion to Maui with certain lady friends, sitting at a bar when a man came up to me and inquired as to whether I'd go to a wedding with him the following day. His closest companion was getting hitched and he required a date. Inside, I heard my specialist urging me to carry on with my life and take risks, so I consented to go. The following morning, I woke up lamenting my choice, however when he called and left a message on my voice message saying he simply required my last name and inquiring as to whether I needed food, fate called and I was submitted. Instinctively, I realized he was the one.

Your qualities are in complete arrangement.

I knew because our perspectives throughout everyday life, our ethics and our way of life simply fit consummately, alongside being head over heels in affection with one another. I felt profoundly enamored and realized I needed to spend a mind-blowing remainder with my accomplice around about fourteen days into dating. We were getting to know each other and the inclination I was encountering was simply unbelievable. Sort of like the maxim, 'When you know, you know.' It felt like I was on some sort of substance that had me happy to the point bursting. I called my closest companion to disclose to her I found my life accomplice and she inquired as to whether I was tanked as a result of the way I was talking and how energized I was via telephone.

You've seen this individual even from a pessimistic standpoint and adore them at any rate.

I met my perfect partner when I was reading for a degree that I despised and my whole life plan was self-destructing. We imparted a level to just the kitchen between us. I didn't understand what had occurred at the time. It wasn't until I took the jump to move home and start from the very beginning again that I understood she was my perfect partner. Someone who saw me for my identity, in the entirety of my catastrophe greatness, and didn't attempt to run. Three years on she's as yet my spirit sister and we experience together and experience new encounters by one another's side as regularly as we can.

You give it a second thought so profoundly about one another that, on occasion, you really sympathize with one another's torment.

I realized I found my perfect partner when his agony turned into my torment. We went to school together and in the middle of classes, we were discussing a relative of his that had as of late entered the emergency clinic. I could tell how disturbed he was and once we gone separate ways, I wound up within a washroom slow down, crying and imploring everything would be alright so he wouldn't need to endure any longer. Understanding that I thought about his family individuals I had never even met as much as my very own family helped me acknowledge how solid my affections for him were.

You feel a sort of power when you contact.

When you meet your perfect partner, you begin to look all starry eyed at automatically, and it's a unique, soul-arousing, knee-debilitating, all-expending worship that will never be copied. You instinctively realize that the individual is a characteristic augmentation of you, suddenly, without exertion, without trade off. The fascination is wild. When you clasp hands, there's a tangible electric flow, there's an ideal fit. The measure of time you've been as one doesn't make a difference, the time you spent separated does.

Your relationship might be rough on occasion yet the unpleasant patches help you develop.

Perfect partners hold up a mirror to us, uncovering such should be recuperated and to be perfectly honest, that is excruciating. Most need to run, which is the reason perfect partner connections will in general be now and again. You separate, you make up, you separate. When you're separated, despite everything it feels like you're as one, on the grounds that vigorously, you are. That feeling of association steps you back together to attempt once more, until it gets agonizing again and the cycle rehashes. Again, and again at times mine included.

You have an inclination that you can allow you to protect down and be 100 percent yourself when you're with this individual.

A perfect partner is your closest companion. Your partner. The one individual your identity happy with demonstrating the odd, clumsy, wound sides of yourself that you more often than not keep covered up around every other person.

You perceive that this individual came into your life to show you a significant exercise.

Your perfect partner is there to be your most noteworthy instructor: the person who difficulties you, makes you insane, blends your most profound interests and touches off your most profound triggers. The perfect partner is the person who difficulties reality of the exercises you need to master with respect to your very own worth, what you need and don't need in life with regards to adore. Tragically, a few people cut off their association with a perfect partner too early considering the battles the experience can bring. Others don't leave the relationship soon enough, so they don't wind up learning the exercise that would have carried them closer to their actual and wanted life mate, which is the thing that we as a whole need and merit.

Meeting your soulmate at the wrong time

Do you know you can meet your soul mate at the wrong time? Here is why.

Science

For what reason would you like somebody who's not directly for you? One reason: science. Ok, that elusive power that makes the very air around you and your nectar shimmer. (At any rate that is the manner by which I imagine science, so go with it.) Masini clarifies, "Having science with somebody is altogether different from having long haul relationship similarity with them. Indeed, you can have extraordinary science with somebody who's not directly for you for twelve distinct reasons." If you're completely spellbound, you may ignore certain issues — like they just escaped a genuine relationship, or they're going to move the nation over. Thus, don't hesitate to fault the flameout of this flame (and my blemished GPA) on science.

Is it accurate to say that we are There Yet?

Timing is everything! Ordinarily individuals, men particularly, conclude that they're prepared to settle down and they do. This could come following 10 years or two of dating, or inside the initial couple of long periods of dating. It normally has to do with a thought of what age you think you need to be before you get hitched, or how a lot of cash you need to make. So, even though you have science and similarity with somebody, in the event that they're not where they figure they ought to be, the planning won't be correct. In some cases, it's only a psychological move of being "prepared" and Masini superbly shows, "It resembles a taxi that turns on its yellow opportunity light. The following individual who banners it down gets the ride!"

Tick Tock: Ladies who need youngsters regularly utilize their natural check to factor in timing. They may feel that they have time on their checks in their mid-20s, yet later, they may feel that it's a great opportunity to accomplice up and make a family. Or flip that around, you may find that your ideal individual needs a family yesterday, however you're not notwithstanding pondering spending your additional salary on anybody yet yourself. In any case, realize that you don't should be seeing someone begin a family, if you are so disposed, you can absolutely approach doing as such without anyone else.

Rebounders: Individuals straight from a separation length the scope of being prepared to hop into another relationship to never needing to be a piece of a "us" again. On the off chance that somebody you're dating is astonishing however shows indications of not being over their ex, notice. A few people feel prepared to supplant their accomplices after a separation or a separation. They're centered on recovering that relationship with another person, and for them, the planning is presently! The inverse can likewise be the reason for relationship death, and it's really no amusing to go separate ways with an extraordinary individual on the grounds that their past relationship still weaving machines the back view reflects. In the event that an individual is bouncing back and you need relationship heartbroken, nectar. Realize that your time is too valuable to even consider wasting on somebody who's pondering another person. You merit the world!

Leave A Light On: I abhor squandering something worth being thankful for, which is maybe why I have a great deal of terminated treats in my ice chest! I asked Masini how she would guide somebody with an instance of "correct individual, wrong time" and she recommends to "be as clear as conceivable with yourself, and your accomplice. Try not to squander your time or theirs. On the off chance that they are never going to profit you need an accomplice to make, and are focused on life as a writer living in a garret, and you need retirement investment funds, kids, a house with a home loan and two vehicles, cut off and proceed onward. Be amenable and kind, yet firm and clear."

Presently, time passes, and individuals change, so you should seriously think about inviting somebody once they've shown signs of improvement place or have settled whatever issue they were pondering. Masini concurs, "You can leave the entryway open — if there are changes. For example, if the artist goes to graduate school and needs to keep in contact, that is a valid justification for keeping the entryway open." Ultimately, I like to feel that when the truly opportune individual appears, the planning will bode well, and I genuinely trust that I for once! won't be late.

What does it feel like meeting your soul mate?

In our way of life and society it is entirely expected to hear the word-perfect partner. Pretty much every lady who has ever begun to look all starry eyed at has called the object of her love her perfect partner. In any case, is it extremely that basic? Is everybody we begin to look all starry eyed at a perfect partner association? What is the distinction between "the one" and your perfect partner? Is it something very similar or is there a noteworthy distinction? Allows find to out.

I think finding your perfect partner is a rare encounter. You just get one perfect partner. They are truly the other portion of you. You just get one other half; you don't get five parts. At times they can be your significant other, yet in any case, together you are entire because the two parts have been joined. When you discover your perfect partner, you are fitting two parts together to make one entirety. You feel a feeling of at long last being finished and discovering your missing piece. Finding your perfect partner can be both a gift and a revile. It's a gift in the event that you meet and remain together, however a revile on the off chance that you meet yet the planning isn't right or different impediments get in your manner and you are compelled to be separated. When you feel that perfect partner association you are never the equivalent again. It is a ground-breaking imperceptible power that solitary you and your other half can feel. I feel it is practically better to never meet your perfect partner at that point to need to meet them and afterward be compelled to part since that can demonstrate to be practically agonizing.

So how would you know whether you've met your actual perfect partner? On the off chance that you need to talk yourself into it or even need to consider it then you know they're not your perfect partner. When you feel a perfect partner association it's moment and you couldn't be more secure with it in your psyche. It resembles you simply know somewhere inside that this specific individual was intended for you and nobody else on the planet. There's no uncertainty or dread in your brain, you have never been more certain about anything in your life like this. When you meet your perfect partner just because, it won't feel like you're simply meeting, you'll feel like you've known them always however simply haven't seen each other for a moment. Your perfect partner will feel extremely recognizable to you even though you've quite recently met. On the off chance that you had no earlier learning of perfect partners, this may be a practically clumsy inclination since you're pondering internally "for what reason does this individual feel so well-known whether we've just barely met?" How can this happen on the grounds that this is reality and not a fantasy. The thing is you simply know. Something within you remembers them path before your brain can completely appreciate it. Your sound personality needs to discover a clarification for it, yet your spirit recognizes what it feels since its other half is found.

CONCLUSION

Thank you for having reached this point in reading, we hope that this text has been useful and therefore able to provide you with the necessary tools to achieve the goal.

The book explained the qualities of a possible soul mate and how to identify her. Many personal peculiarities can become challenges for your ideal relationship if they are not investigated. The book has covered in depth the decisions that influence the choice of a partner. In addition, there are some individual features that complicate a possible relationship before it becomes real.

The text considered communication as a crucial factor in a relationship. Remember that communication is two-way. A relationship should have both partners working for a successful union. When you find yourself working alone for this end take a step back and think. Although apparently ideal may not be the right partner.

Finally, the book has told you the things that can end the report. Finding a soul mate doesn't mean you'll relax; there will be challenges and you'll have to work on them every day. He also told you how to behave when you think you've found a possible soul mate.

The next step is to practice what you have read. When you have met your potential partner, take note of the guidelines. Don't be too serious in trying to reach everything right away. Stay rational and take it one step at a time.

The book has explained on the qualities of a soul mate and how you will identify them. There is also an in depth of the boundaries that may bring challenges to your relationship if they are not investigated. The book has covered with in depth the decisions that influence your choice of a partner. Further, there are some individual characteristics that complicate a relationship before it is official. The book has covered that among other reasons that bring challenges in a relationship.

The book has looked at communication as a crucial factor in a relationship. While building one, remember that communication is two way. A relationship should have both partners working towards having a successful union. When you find yourself working on it alone, take a step back and reflect about it. It just may not be the right one.

Finally, the book has told you about the things that may end the relationship. Finding a soul mate does not mean that you will relax; there will be challenges and you must work on it daily. It has also told you how to behave when you find a soul mate.

The next step is to practice what you have read. When you have met your potential partner, take note of the guidelines set in these books. Don't be too serious about achieving it all at once. Be cool and implement one step at a time.

All the best as you look to meet your soul mate.

(Finally, if you found this book useful in any way, a review on Amazon is always appreciated!)